On the cover: Nicole Reding as Vittoria
Photo by Craig Schwartz

I Gelosi
© David Bridel
Trade Edition, 2014
ISBN 978-1-934962-39-8

Sublimity

Synopsis: SUBLIMITY investigates the life of tormented English poet Samuel Taylor Coleridge, focusing on the fateful evening in 1797 when he composed his famous pre-romantic masterpiece, Kubla Khan. The tragicomic character of Coleridge - part tender fool, part opium addict - embodies a restless search to understand the nature of creativity and inspiration.

Cast Size: 1 Male

I GELOSI
By David Bridel

I GELOSI was first performed with the MFA acting students at UCLA in 2006 with the following cast:

FRANCESCO ANDREINI - Jason Greenfield
GUILIO PASQUATI - Paul Moore
SIMONE DI BOLOGNA - Dorian Logan
ORAZIO PADOVANO - Shawn Colten
ISABELLA ANDREINI - Amy Rush
VITTORIA PIISSIMI - Nicole Reding
SYLVIA - Emily Rose
VINCENZO, DUKE OF MANTUA - Kahlil Joseph
CHARLES IX, KING OF FRANCE - Sergio Savinov
CATHERINE DE MEDICI - Jamaica Perry
DEGRISE - Matt Weedman

Thanks to Mel Shapiro.

I GELOSI was professionally staged at the Los Angeles Theatre Ensemble in 2008 with the following cast:

FRANCESCO ANDREINI - Albert Meijer
GUILIO PASQUATI - Isaac Wade
SIMONE DI BOLOGNA - Michael John Pappas
ORAZIO PADOVANO - Jon Redding
ISABELLA ANDREINI - Paige Lindsey White
VITTORIA PIISSIMI - Eleanor Van Hest
SYLVIA - Emily Rose/Catherine Talton
VINCENZO, DUKE OF MANTUA - Christopher Tillman
CHARLES IX, KING OF FRANCE - Luke Bailey
CATHERINE DE MEDICI - Danielle Katz

Thanks to Tom Burmester.

CHARACTERS

FRANCESCO ANDREINI (male, 30's)
GUILIO PASQUATI (male, 30's)
SIMONE DI BOLOGNA (male, 30's)
ORAZIO PADOVANO (male, 20's)
ISABELLA ANDREINI (female, 20's)
VITTORIA PIISSIMI (female, 30's)
SYLVIA (female, 20's)
VINCENZO, DUKE OF MANTUA (male, 40's)
CHARLES IX, KING OF FRANCE (male, 20's)
CATHERINE DE MEDICI (female, 50's)

Some voices, guards, etc

The action takes place in the latter half of the 16th Century

Place: Italy, France

I GELOSI

PROLOGUE

(The company Gelosi - Francesco, Isabella, Guilio, Simone in a skirt, Orazio, Vittoria, Sylvia - are chatting idly while the audience takes their seats. Throughout the entire play these seven characters will never leave the playing space. When not in a scene, each has their own area at the side or back of the stage where they wait, drink or attend to small matters, and watch the action unfold. Francesco and Isabella come forward to address the audience. The company joins them at the front of the stage.)

FRANCESCO: Signori, my name is Francesco Andreini, and I am dead. This is my wife:

ISABELLA: Isabella Andreini. I am also dead.

FRANCESCO: This is our company of actors. The Gelosi. They're all dead too. Everyone here has been dead for several hundred years. Now let's put that behind us, and we'll show you what we can do.

(Francesco and Isabella clap their hands. The company brings out musical instruments and play. They clap again. Various acrobatics.)

FRANCESCO: Tragedy, pastoral, comedy, the Gelosi does it all. Guilio here can improvise in four languages. Orazio extemporizes verse at the drop of a hat. Vittoria can make an audience fall in love with her in the flash of an eye. And my wife... My wife can appear before you stark raving mad, and you won't know whether she's pretending or not. The Gelosi.

ISABELLA: We were the first.

FRANCESCO: We were the greatest.

ISABELLA: In Paris, they spoke of us for hundreds of years.

FRANCESCO: We came from all over Italy to perform for one purpose alone.

GUILIO: Profit.

VITTORIA: Fame.

ORAZIO: Love.

SIMONE: Food.

SYLVIA: Rebellion.

ISABELLA: Poetry.

FRANCESCO: Revenge. We came for revenge.

(Disagreement among all.)

FRANCESCO: We're going to tell you our story.

ISABELLA: You'll meet Kings and Dukes and hang-men.

FRANCESCO: You'll witness adultery.

ISABELLA: You'll marvel at true love.

FRANCESCO: And when you leave the theater tonight, you will crave one thing, and one thing alone.

GUILIO: Profit.

VITTORIA: Fame.

ORAZIO: Love.

SIMONE: Food.

SYLVIA: Rebellion.

ISABELLA: Poetry.

FRANCESCO: Revenge.

(Disagreement among all.)

FRANCESCO: Places, everyone, we mustn't keep them
waiting.

(The company drift off to prepare.)

SIMONE: My bones ache.

FRANCESCO: It is March, 1568. The scene is Milan. It
is six months since we were liberated from the Holy
Wars and returned home to form the Gelosi. It is not a
glamorous life. We do skits and farces outdoors to
passers-by. We don't have two coins to rub together.
These are desperate times. But I am about to have an
idea that will change the theatre forever.

ISABELLA: What did you say?

FRANCESCO: I said I am about to have an idea that
will change the theatre forever.

ISABELLA: It was your idea?

FRANCESCO: Of course it was my idea.

VITTORIA: I think it was her idea, sweetie.

ORAZIO: It was her idea.

FRANCESCO: Excuse me – neither of you were there –
Guilio, whose idea was it?

GUILIO: It was our idea, actually.

FRANCESCO: Our idea?

GUILIO: Yours and mine.

FRANCESCO: No it wasn't.

ISABELLA: You're both wrong.

(Disagreement among all.)

FRANCESCO: All right, that's enough. *We* are about to
have an idea that will change the theatre forever. Satisfied? *(To audience)* My apologies. *(To Gelosi)* Are
we ready?

(Mutterings of consent.)

FRANCESCO: It is 1568. Begin!

(Francesco and Isabella clap their hands.)

PART 1 - ITALY

1. THE GRAND IDEA

(Guilio and Simone are rehearsing a scene.)

PANTALONE (GUILIO): *'Flaminia? Won't you stand a little closer, my precious Flaminia?'*

FLAMINIA (SIMONE): *'Oh Pantalone. I don't know if I should.'*

PANTALONE (GUILIO): *'Give me a kiss, my sweet little Flaminia.'*

FRANCESCO: *(interrupting)* Just a moment. Simone, what's the matter?

SIMONE: Nothing.

FRANCESCO: You're supposed to kiss him, not sniff him. Try again.

PANTALONE (GUILIO): *'Flaminia? Won't you stand a little closer, my precious Flaminia?'*

FLAMINIA (SIMONE): *'Oh Pantalone. I don't know if I should.'*

PANTALONE (GUILIO): *'Give me a kiss, my sweet little Flaminia.'*

FRANCESCO: You did it again.

SIMONE: I can't help it. He smells of garlic.

GUILIO: I don't.

SIMONE: Yes you do. It makes me hungry. I can't concentrate.

FRANCESCO: You have to stop thinking about your stomach.

SIMONE: When's lunch?

GUILIO: We ate lunch.

SIMONE: What did we have?

GUILIO: We shared an apple.

SIMONE: When's dinner?

FRANCESCO: Simone. If this scene isn't funny, there won't be any dinner. And there won't be any breakfast tomorrow. How many coins do we have left, Guilio?

GUILIO: Three.

FRANCESCO: Three coins left. We're about to go broke.

SIMONE: We're always about to go broke. I'm sick of this life. I want to go back to Bologna. My mother makes a rabbit pie to die for. I used to eat it on the steps. A pretty girl wanders past. Hello! Can I sing you a song?

FRANCESCO: Rehearsal.

SIMONE: All right, all right.

(They are about to begin.)

SIMONE: You know she's watching us again. Over there.

FRANCESCO: Never mind her.

SIMONE: Every day, rain or shine. I think she's got a crush on you.

FRANCESCO: Lots of girls have crushes on me, it's not important.

SIMONE: She'll get into trouble if she isn't careful... *(Calling out)* Shoo! Go on, this is no place for you. You're too young and too pretty to mix with the likes of us. *(Turns back)* I think she's listening.

GUILIO: Simone, will you shut up? We have to rehearse. We have to be funnier. We have to draw bigger crowds. I refuse to scrounge around like this for the rest of my life.

SIMONE: You see? You're sick of it too. This is worse than the army. Six years in a Turkish prison was better than six months as a player. Somebody threw a stone at me yesterday and yelled 'Show us your tits!'

FRANCESCO: Rehearsal.

SIMONE: All right, all right.

(They are about to begin.)

SIMONE: Why is it always me that has to dress up as the woman? Every play that we do I have to be the woman. I'm your lover. I'm his lover. I marry you. I marry him. This old skirt is getting raggedy. I want to play in a mask.

FRANCESCO: There aren't any stories with three men and no women.

SIMONE: But I look so ridiculous.

FRANCESCO: You're supposed to look ridiculous. Ridiculous is funny. Ridiculous is big crowds. Ridiculous is money in hat. It is necessary that you look ridiculous.

SIMONE: And you told me playing would give me back my self-respect.

FRANCESCO: It will. Be patient. First we have to make our mark, and Rome wasn't built in a day. So put that skirt back on and show us your tits.

SIMONE: Hey. If we only had an apple for lunch, how come you stink of garlic?

GUILIO: I don't stink of garlic.

SIMONE: Have you been eating pie?

GUILIO: What pie?

SIMONE: Any kind of pie. Pie with garlic in it.

GUILIO: I don't know what you're talking about.

FRANCESCO: So he had some pie, what's the difference?

13

SIMONE: He did have some pie?

GUILIO: I did not have any pie.

(Simone is taking off his skirt.)

SIMONE: Right. That is it. I'm not going on.

FRANCESCO: What?

SIMONE: I'm not going on. I'm hungry, you bastard. We're supposed to share everything.

GUILIO: I'm telling you I did not have any pie.

(Francesco draws his sword.)

FRANCESCO: Get back in that skirt and rehearse.

SIMONE: Oh, so that's how you treat me, is it?

FRANCESCO: Get back in that skirt, fool, or I will run you through with pleasure.

GUILIO: Hey, Cesco, calm down.

SIMONE: Go on then, kill me. I hope I go to hell, it can't be any worse than this.

FRANCESCO: You are an ungrateful little shit – I ought to carve my name on your balls.

GUILIO: Hey, hey, hey. Cut it out.

SIMONE: For six months we've been wasting our time. We're penniless, we're starving, and our play is a joke. I quit.

(He throws down the skirt. Isabella enters.)

ISABELLA: Signori. This is the boldest moment of my life. I have watched your performances ever since you arrived in Milan, I have watched them faithfully, if you will forgive me, and I do believe that you are, all three of you, most excellent players with the finest timing and the most diverting senses of humor... And yet – far be it from me, a mere face in the crowd - and yet I cannot help but wonder whether a little, and I mean a fraction, more of the Lyrical would serve your purposes well; for an audience, though easily reduced to fits at the sight and sound of frolicking, also has, though it may not know it itself, a higher purpose, a desire to be enlightened, transported, I believe, by a discipline that could be dearly executed by the right player on the right stage - I speak of poetry. I contend, signori, there is a seed within the human heart that only poetry can nurture, and its growth and flowering is the wish, however distant and unknown, of every humble crowd that gathers about the trestle.

SIMONE: Oh she's beautiful.

ISABELLA: To that end, signori, though I hardly dare to confess it, I have here composed a speech for your play, and humbly I offer it to you as a token of my admiration. It is for the buffoon who portrays the woman.

(She hands a parchment to Simone.)

SIMONE: I can't read.

ISABELLA: Perhaps the signore will read it for you.

15

(Simone hands the parchment to Francesco.)

FRANCESCO: *(reads)*
'Though woman is mere flesh and blood,
Her heart is a star; it follows a course
In the skies. You cannot capture this heart
Unless you, too, leave the earth behind,
As if in a dream. This is the impossible truth,
Delivered in the language of truth; a poem.'
(to Isabella)
What is your name?

ISABELLA: Isabella Canali, signore.

GUILIO: Guilio Pasquati, at your service. This is Simone di Bologna.

FRANCESCO: Where did you learn to compose like this?

ISABELLA: The poetry composes itself, signore. I am merely the messenger.

FRANCESCO: Do you live here in Milan?

ISABELLA: Yes, but my father does not know I am talking with you. He disapproves of players.

SIMONE: Signorina, your speech is a marvel. But I could never learn it, I have no more brain than a sausage. Besides, I'm going back to Bologna. The Gelosi has lost its only woman.

(Francesco and Guilio are studying Simone's skirt.)

FRANCESCO: The right player...

GUILIO: On the right stage.

(Francesco takes Guilio aside. Simone follows.)

FRANCESCO: Are you thinking what I'm thinking?

GUILIO: People will come from all over Milan.

SIMONE: What's going on? Who's thinking what?

FRANCESCO: They'll come from all over the country.

GUILIO: We'll be playing to thousands within a week.

FRANCESCO: It's audacious.

GUILIO: It's unprecedented.

SIMONE: Hey. You're not thinking – Cesco, no. Have you gone out of your mind? A woman on the stage? It's madness. We'll be kicked out of Milan.

FRANCESCO: Then we'll go somewhere else.

SIMONE: What if the church hears about this?

FRANCESCO: I don't give a damn about the church.

(They return to Isabella.)

FRANCESCO: Signorina, we have discussed your offer carefully, and we are delighted to insert your verses into our play, on one condition. You will deliver the speech yourself. You, signorina, will play the woman in our play.

ISABELLA: Oh – signore –

SIMONE: Hey. Who am I going to play? If she plays the woman, who am I going to play?

GUILIO: I thought you quit.

SIMONE: Yes, but that was – not any more – you didn't believe me, did you?

FRANCESCO: You can play in a mask.

SIMONE: Now you're talking.

2. THE OPPORTUNITY

(In the market square. The following 'scene' from the Gelosi's play is performed with the actors facing upstage, silhouetted, perhaps, against a stage curtain. Downstage of the curtain are Francesco and Simone – until he enters the play.)

PANTALONE (GUILIO): *'Isabella? Won't you stand a little closer, my precious Isabella?'*

ISABELLA: *'Oh Pantalone. I don't know if I should...'*

PANTALONE (GUILIO): *'Give me a kiss, my sweet little Isabella.'*

ISABELLA: *'Only if you answer me this riddle.'*

PANTALONE (GUILIO): *'Arlecchino!'*

ARLECCHINO (SIMONE) *(in mask, entering)*: 'Signore?'

PANTALONE (GUILIO): *'Help me answer this riddle, or I'll knock you into next week.'*

ARLECCHINO (SIMONE): *'Yes, signore!'*

ISABELLA: *'I am strong, but you think I am weak. I am bold but you think I am shy. I am old but you think I am young. Now guess who I am in one try.'*

PANTALONE (GUILIO): *'One try – ah, we'd better think carefully, Arlecchino, we only have one try. Don't be rash, don't be rash, let us ponder this riddle...'*

ARLECCHINO (SIMONE): *'A chicken!'*

PANTALONE (GUILIO): *'A chicken? What kind of idiot would think of a chicken?'*

ARLECCHINO (SIMONE): *'Chickens are strong...'* (He wrestles with a powerful imaginary chicken.) *'Chickens are shy...'* (He calls an elusive imaginary chicken.) *'Chickens are old – oh, no they're not. They're chickens.'*

PANTALONE (GUILIO): *'You've ruined my chance of a kiss, you numbskull, you half-wit, you Turk-brain...'*

(Pantalone chases Arlecchino 'off'. They arrive downstage of the curtain and congratulate one another on a successful performance as Isabella finishes the play.)

ISABELLA:
'Though woman is mere flesh and blood,
Her heart is a star; it follows a course
In the skies. You cannot capture this heart
Unless you, too, leave the earth behind,
As if in a dream. This is the impossible truth,
Delivered in the language of truth; our play.'

(Keen applause. Backstage:)

GUILIO: (counting money from hat) Two hundred and twelve... two thirteen...

SIMONE: Today, lamb stew with Tuscan potatoes.

GUILIO: Two fourteen... two fifteen...

SIMONE: And a bottle of French wine. Our luck has officially changed.

GUILIO: Luck had nothing to do with it - it was a business decision and a very astute one.

SIMONE: The signorina has a magic touch. Such grace, such beauty was never seen before on a stage. And she writes like a true poet. Even Francesco is impressed, aren't you, Cesco?

FRANCESCO: Hmm?

SIMONE: On Tuesday I saw him kissing her behind the vegetable stand.

FRANCESCO: As a matter of fact, she was kissing me.

SIMONE: Oh, well that's different.

GUILIO: Two hundred and twenty four coins. That's our best yet. Makes our total for the fortnight seven hundred and thirty eight. At this rate with, say, eleven performances a week, our annual income will be three thousand coins.

SIMONE: I'm going to buy a villa. My mother will come and live with me. Casa Simone.

FRANCESCO: Before anyone draws a wage we have to attend to company expenses.

GUILIO: New props.

FRANCESCO: Paint the wagon.

GUILIO: A horse of our own, for travel.

SIMONE: Travel? Where are we going?

FRANCESCO: We're going to take this show to the provinces.

GUILIO: More towns, more money.

SIMONE: But if we leave Milan, what will happen to the signorina? She can't start traveling with a bunch of players. She'll be disgraced.

FRANCESCO: The thought had occurred to me.

SIMONE: And without her we'll be back where we started.

GUILIO: Which is not an option.

FRANCESCO: Thus it is, dear Simone, that you will be amazed at the solution we have come up with. Yesterday evening, after the performance, I married Isabella.

SIMONE: What?

FRANCESCO: A fleeting glance, a stolen kiss, a trip to the priest –

GUILIO: One witness.

FRANCESCO: And presto. She can leave home with head held high. She's collecting her things as we speak.

SIMONE: But you've only known her two weeks.

FRANCESCO: You said it yourself. We can't leave her behind.

SIMONE: Yesterday evening?

GUILIO: You were eating a pie.

SIMONE: But Francesco – the girl is mad about you.

FRANCESCO: Yes; that helped.

SIMONE: But do you love her?

GUILIO: Ha! Listen to him.

SIMONE: Love is important.

GUILIO: Strategy is the only important thing in life.

(Isabella enters, with traveling bags.)

ISABELLA: Francesco.

FRANCESCO: Darling.

ISABELLA: When I told my father that I had married one of the players from the piazza he threatened to beat me. When I told him that I had been appearing on the stage for two weeks already he called me a harlot and tried to lock me in my bedroom. But I escaped through the window and climbed down the pear tree. I have my quill and my parchment – I'm free. This is the happiest day of my life.

GUILIO: An official welcome to the Gelosi – signora.

ISABELLA: Thank you, Guilio.

SIMONE: Allow me to wish you every good fortune, signora. You'll need it.

(Orazio approaches.)

ORAZIO: Excuse me, signori. You are the company Gelosi, the talk of all Milan?

FRANCESCO: We are.

ORAZIO: Orazio Padovano, at your service. I wish to speak with the signorina, if I may.

FRANCESCO: The signora. Signora Isabella Andreini, my wife.

ORAZIO: Signora. I wish to compliment you on the exquisiteness of your verse. I have seen many performances in my time; I am an afficionado of the stage; I contend that no other player has ever matched your delicacy. Then, of course, no other player shares your advantages...

ISABELLA: Thank you, signore.

ORAZIO: Heartbreak brought me to this city; but my heart has been replenished by your performance. I can live again.

ISABELLA: Thank you again, signore.

ORAZIO: And now, without further ado, I would like to request that I join your company. It is not an easy path to tread, I know. Many years of hard graft lie ahead, and the small fragments of inspiration are outweighed by the chronic burden of poverty. Nevertheless, I want to be a player. I have had some experience performing. My uncle has a soft spot for the spoken word, and I have read much of Horace aloud at certain parties, with fellow students, in the lilac gardens, and I have been told perchance that I have a mellifluous delivery. I have prepared a short piece; a snippet, if you will. I'll stand over here, shall I? Oh! I'm nervous. I'm just an amateur. Here, then, is my piece:

'My heart is like the anvil that resists the hammer-stroke
Of your obstinacy. My breast is marble to withstand your fire;
My bosom is ice, ice so hard your flames cannot melt it,
And you are a fury for my torment in the realms of love.
Argh! I suffer. Argh! I weep. Argh!
Love is a star; a star is born; you have from me my poor heart torn.'

(The Gelosi applaud Orazio, uncertainly.)

ORAZIO: Thank you. I think I might have missed the true passion of the last two lines -

FRANCESCO: Signore, we are honored that you consider us worthy of your talents. However, we are a small company, as you see, and we're very sorry...

ORAZIO: *(he has become emotional)* Oh dear – I promised myself I wouldn't cry. Speaking as one whose very soul has been shredded, torn asunder by the hardships of love - I've never felt so liberated - reciting before the famous Gelosi... My uncle won't believe it when I tell him. He's got a soft spot for the stage, you know.

FRANCESCO: Yes. Anyway, we're very sorry...

ORAZIO: It was uncle who advised me to travel, when he saw how my heart had been crushed. I believe that I owe him my life. He's the Duke of Mantua.

(Pause.)

FRANCESCO: Your uncle is the Duke of Mantua?

ORAZIO: A man of culture. A man of sophistication. A man who loves nothing more than a great feast, with wine, and meats, and warm cheese, and a play to follow. You were saying?

FRANCESCO: What?

ORAZIO: You were saying you're very sorry...

FRANCESCO: We're very sorry...

GUILIO: We're very sorry that we didn't meet you earlier.

FRANCESCO: Very sorry.

GUILIO: Because you will make a wonderful addition to our ranks.

FRANCESCO: Welcome to the Gelosi.

ORAZIO: Oh sir - I am overcome...

FRANCESCO: And the timing could not be better. We leave for Mantua tomorrow!

GUILIO: Tomorrow.

ORAZIO: For Mantua? Tomorrow?

FRANCESCO: I assume your uncle can be persuaded to receive us?

ORAZIO: Oh - I am sure he can, but...

FRANCESCO: Excellent. Then send word of our impending arrival.

ISABELLA: What is it, Orazio?

ORAZIO: Oh dear. My poor heart... You see, I left Mantua because of - because of a woman...

FRANCESCO: Signore. Fear no women. You are Gelosi now.

ORAZIO: Gelosi... Yes... So I am...

GUILIO: Have confidence, signore.

ORAZIO: Yes - yes, I will have confidence. I am Gelosi. I am Gelosi.

SIMONE: Are we sure this is a good idea?

3. THE PATRON

(In Mantua, in front of the Duke. As before, the play is performed at the rear, in silhouette.)

ISABELLA: *'Now guess who I am in one try.'*

PANTALONE (GUILIO): *'One try – ah, we'd better think carefully, Arlecchino, we only have one try. Don't be rash, don't be rash, let us ponder this riddle…'*

ARLECCHINO (SIMONE): *'A chicken!'*

PANTALONE (GUILIO): *'A chicken? What kind of idiot would think of a chicken?'*

ARLECCHINO (SIMONE): *'Chickens are strong…'* (He wrestles with a powerful imaginary chicken.) *'Chickens are shy… '(He calls an elusive imaginary chicken) 'Chickens are old – oh, no they're not. They're chickens.'*

LEANDRO (ORAZIO): *(entering)* 'I know the answer!'

ISABELLA: *'Leandro!'*

LEANDRO (ORAZIO): *'I have heard of this riddle. I shall solve it, and claim your kiss as reward. The answer is –'*

(He goes up on his line.)

LEANDRO (ORAZIO): *'The answer is –'*

(Nothing. Francesco, from backstage, prompts him desperately, to no avail.)

ISABELLA: *(covering)* 'I'm also mindful of my duty /
But you love me for my beauty.'

(Still nothing.)

ISABELLA: *'Though I'm modest don't dismiss me / I'm
not modest when you kiss me./ Can you guess yet? I'll
reprieve you / And my verse will not deceive you /
Follow, and you will not tell a / Lie when you say…'*

LEANDRO (ORAZIO): *'Isabella! You!'*

(Isabella and Leandro kiss.)

PANTALONE (GUILIO): *'You ruined my chance of a
kiss, you numbskull, you half-wit, you Turk-brain…'*

(Pantalone chases Arlecchino off.)

ISABELLA:
  'Though woman is mere flesh and blood,
  Her heart is a star; it follows a course
  In the skies. You cannot capture this heart
  Unless you, too, leave the earth behind,
  As if in a dream. This is the impossible truth,
  Delivered in the language of truth; our play.'

(Keen applause. Backstage:)

ORAZIO: I thought perhaps I was a little nervous…

FRANCESCO: Maybe a little.

ORAZIO: But your wife kept the inspiration alive.

FRANCESCO: We are all indebted to my wife. Gelosi,
bravo. Even you, you old goat.

GUILIO: Thanks.

FRANCESCO: He just needs a bit more rehearsal.

SIMONE: I've never performed inside in my life. We don't even have to hold out our hats. Who was that big fellow in the front row? Couldn't stop chuckling.

ORAZIO: That was my uncle.

(Enter the Duke of Mantua.)

DUKE: May I offer my sincerest congratulations to the company Gelosi.

ORAZIO: Hello uncle.

DUKE: Orazio. An unforgettable debut. Your wages, signori.

(The Duke gives a bag of money to Francesco.)

FRANCESCO: We are your grateful servants, signore.

(Francesco tosses the money to Guilio.)

DUKE: I must kiss the hand of this magnificent creature. Some of us were a little skeptical when we heard that a woman was to play. You have proved a great many nobles wrong, signora. Yours was an illustrious display of the heart.

ISABELLA: My heart is full of love, signore.

DUKE: So I see, so I see. Your success has made some of our women quite jealous too.

ISABELLA: That was not my intention, signore.

DUKE: Of course not. Signora, signori. Make yourselves at home, please, for the rest of the evening,
there is plenty of food and wine.

(He exits. He returns.)

DUKE: Oh! One other thing: I have a business proposition for you.

FRANCESCO: What's that?

DUKE: I have heard that the Duke of Venice is adopt-
ing a theater company as his own. I have decided I
would like to do the same. If you agreed, you would
play in Mantua at my command. Six weeks in the
Spring, six weeks in the Autumn. At other times you
would be my ambassadors abroad. I've had a contract
drawn up. See what you think.

(He exits, leaving the contract with Francesco.)

FRANCESCO: *(reading)* 'On the day of Mercury, 25th
of the month, at the Palazzo of Vincenzo, 12th Duke
of Mantua. Clause 1. We the undersigned compan-
ions, collectively known as the Gelosi, agree to form
a company of players under the patronage of the
aforesaid Duke of Mantua, for such time as both parties find it mutually convenient. Clause 2. The Duke
hereby agrees to pay the Gelosi the sum of one thousand coins a month' – one thousand coins! – 'until
such time as this contract is declared null and void...
Clause 3. The company may decide internal conflicts
by means of the majority... Clause 4,5, 6...'

(He turns the pages.)

FRANCESCO: '15, 30' – it's very thorough. It's going to take all night to read.

GUILIO: Patronage. Patronage, Cesco!

ORAZIO: I knew uncle would come up trumps.

FRANCESCO: We sign.

SIMONE: I can't write.

FRANCESCO: Put a cross.

(They sign. The Duke enters.)

DUKE: And what have we decided?

FRANCESCO: We have decided to accept your most generous offer, signore.

DUKE: Excellent. I will look after the Gelosi, and you will perform for the glory of Mantua. It will be mutually beneficent. Next week, as it happens, Mantua plays host to His Serene Majesty Charles, King of France, and his mother Catherine, of Medici. The King is a discerning theater-goer; I shall offer them a command performance.

FRANCESCO: We are going to play to the King of France?

DUKE: Precisely. Now rest well and eat well. I want you in top form for the King.

(He exits. He returns.)

DUKE: Oh! One other thing. As permitted by the terms of the contract, I have decided to add one to your number. A new player awaits.

FRANCESCO: What?

DUKE: Clause 33. Decisions regarding the hire and release of company members rest with the patron. You won't be disappointed. You can come in now, peachblossom...

(Vittoria enters.)

DUKE: Signora, Signori. Allow me to introduce Signorina Vittoria Piissimi of Padua.

VITTORIA: Good evening.

SIMONE: Oh she's naughty.

VITTORIA: Thank you, Vincenzo. I can manage from here.

DUKE: I'll leave you to it, then. Signora, signori. Peachblossom.

(He exits. Vittoria goes straight to Isabella.)

VITTORIA: Signora. Please accept my compliments on a magnificent performance. I was deeply moved.

ISABELLA: Thank you, signorina. I am honored to have impressed one as beautiful as you.

(Vittoria goes to Francesco.)

VITTORIA: Signore. You have made a modest woman blush, and blush again.

FRANCESCO: Delighted, signorina.

(Vittoria goes to Guilio and Simone.)

VITTORIA: You, signori, are the essence of comedy.

GUILIO: We aim to please.

(Vittoria goes to Orazio.)

VITTORIA: Signore Orazio.

(Orazio starts crying.)

FRANCESCO: What's the matter with him?

(Orazio is pointing at Vittoria.)

ISABELLA: Oh no...

VITTORIA: I am told that I have no lack of talent, and I am prepared to work hard. On stage, I believe I will complement your company beautifully. Above all else, I can look after myself and I won't meddle in any of your affairs. And now, signori, signora, I believe we have the honor of playing to royalty next week: shall we rehearse?

4. THE ACTRESS

(In the foreground, Guilio is counting money. Simone is asleep. Isabella is writing. In the background, sounds of a rehearsal.)

ISABELLA: I'll wear a hole in this parchment if I'm not careful. I can't seem to write them down fast enough.

(No reply.)

ISABELLA: Verses. For the King. I'm writing a new epilogue.

GUILIO: Hmm?

ISABELLA: For the King of France.

GUILIO: Yes.

ISABELLA: One day I hope that my plays will be published by the Academy of Letters. It's my secret vanity. My father told me hell would freeze over before a woman was published.

(Pause.)

ISABELLA: Guilio?

GUILIO: Yes?

ISABELLA: Tell me, have you and my husband always been so single-minded?

GUILIO: Single minded?

ISABELLA: In your ambitions.

GUILIO: We just want to make a good life for ourselves.

ISABELLA: You fought in the Holy Wars together, didn't you?

GUILIO: Pope Gregory's army.

ISABELLA: And you were captured by the Turks?

GUILIO: Six years.

ISABELLA: Francesco doesn't tell me anything about it.

GUILIO: Perhaps he doesn't remember.

ISABELLA: Oh, I have a feeling he remembers.

GUILIO: They kept us in a prison in the middle of the desert. They starved us within an inch of our lives. They strapped us to the walls for weeks at a time while the rats ate the slop in our bowls. They boiled lamb outside our window till we began screaming at the smell. One night Francesco dreamed he was eating a fresh peach. When he woke up he had gnawed his fist to the bone. Perhaps he doesn't want to remember.

ISABELLA: No.

GUILIO: It's all behind us now, anyway. We have a new life.

ISABELLA: I wake up at night and he's sitting on the edge of the bed, talking to himself. I think he's plotting something.

GUILIO: Plotting something? There's nothing to plot.

(Francesco arrives.)

FRANCESCO: Guilio, your turn to rehearse.

GUILIO: We're up five hundred and seventy seven coins. After expenses.

FRANCESCO: Perfect.

GUILIO: Is she good?

FRANCESCO: She will serve our purposes perfectly.

GUILIO: One woman was a sensation; two will be a scandal.

(Guilio goes to rehearse with Vittoria.)

ISABELLA: What are our purposes, by the way?

FRANCESCO: To please the King, of course.

ISABELLA: Of course. I've been writing a new epilogue.

FRANCESCO: Hmm? Good.

ISABELLA: One day I hope my plays will be published. It's my -

FRANCESCO: Yes.

ISABELLA: Francesco..?

FRANCESCO: What is it?

ISABELLA: There's nobody here.

FRANCESCO: Simone's here.

ISABELLA: He's asleep.

FRANCESCO: I should wake him up. He needs to rehearse with her too -

ISABELLA: Now would be a good time to kiss me.

FRANCESCO: Come here.

(They kiss.)

ISABELLA: Are you happy with me, Cesco?

FRANCESCO: Yes. This is my disposition. You'll get used to it

ISABELLA: We still don't know each other very well, do we?

FRANCESCO: I know that you're pretty.

ISABELLA: Don't you want to learn about me, Francesco?

FRANCESCO: Of course I do.

ISABELLA: Then ask me a question.

FRANCESCO: What's your favorite color?

ISABELLA: That's not a question.

FRANCESCO: Yes it is a question.

ISABELLA: Ask me what the stage is for.

FRANCESCO: What..?

ISABELLA: We're going to live our lives on it, we should at least have an opinion. I believe that the stage is for the expression of all that is beautiful in life. I'm not saying there's no room for suffering on stage - in fact, it's not much of a show if somebody doesn't suffer, and preferably at length. Suffering is beautiful, in any case, and so is anguish. But as for loathing, and bitterness... I don't think they belong on the stage at all. What do you think?

FRANCESCO: All I ever do is play the fool. I want people to laugh, there's no bitterness in that.

ISABELLA: I'm speaking of your plans, Francesco.

FRANCESCO: What plans?

ISABELLA: You talk in your sleep.

FRANCESCO: What do I say?

ISABELLA: Ambush.

FRANCESCO: I must be thinking about the wars.

(Simone wakes with a start.)

SIMONE: Ah!

FRANCESCO: What is it?

SIMONE: I was about to be hanged.

(Sylvia, the Duke's maid, enters.)

SYLVIA: Everyone got everything they need?

(They look at her.)

SYLVIA: I'm the new maid. The other one got dropsy. Everyone got everything they need?

(Pause.)

SYLVIA: All right, don't all shout at once.

(She goes.)

SIMONE: Oh she's magnificent.

(Guilio enters.)

GUILIO: Simone. Your turn to rehearse.

SIMONE: I could take her to the moon. Come, pretty one, the moon is made of cheese…

GUILIO: Simone. Did you hear what I said?

(Orazio enters.)

ORAZIO: Signori, Signora, I'm afraid I must hurriedly announce my resignation from the company Gelosi. I have a cousin in Pisa who is very sick. He has been bitten by a venomous Norwegian spider.

FRANCESCO: Signore.

ORAZIO: It was a great pleasure to know you all –

FRANCESCO: Signore Orazio.

ORAZIO: And I hope that in the future our paths may cross -

FRANCESCO: Signore! The Gelosi plays to the King of France in two days.

ORAZIO: I know.

GUILIO: You're not getting as far as the street, let alone Pisa.

ORAZIO: But my cousin – the spider -

FRANCESCO: This has nothing to do with your cousin. You're scared of that woman.

ORAZIO: She has crushed my heart. She is a monster. She devours a man, until there is nothing left, not even a shell, a husk. I must leave the Gelosi.

GUILIO: You've signed a contract. You stay.

ORAZIO: I'm sorry signori. I go.

FRANCESCO: *(drawing sword)* You stay, or I will carve my name on your balls.

GUILIO: Cesco, careful.

ORAZIO: You can't make me.

ISABELLA: Francesco, put that thing away.

FRANCESCO: You stay!

ORAZIO: This isn't fair!

(Fracas. The Duke enters.)

DUKE: Gelosi! What is the meaning of this?

FRANCESCO: A minor disturbance.

DUKE: You are not paid to squabble. You are paid to rehearse. You have a very important performance ahead of you.

GUILIO: It won't happen again, Signore Duke.

DUKE: There are other companies, you know. I hear the Fortunati are looking for a patron. And a new leading lady. I am sure Signorina Piissimi would be to their taste.

FRANCESCO: Nothing to worry about, Signore Duke. We are delighted to have the Signorina with us. She is proving to be an admirable player.

DUKE: She is a peachblossom.

(Vittoria enters.)

VITTORIA: Signora, I've been thinking that perhaps I should deliver the new epilogue to the King. A fresh face. What do you think, Vincenzo?

DUKE: An excellent idea.

43

5. THE KING AND HIS MOTHER

(Vittoria is delivering the epilogue to the King of France. The rest of the company wait backstage.)

VITTORIA:
  'You cannot capture our hearts
  Unless you, too, leave the earth behind,
  As if in a dream, a slow dream; it is the one
  Condition of love. This is the impossible truth,
  Delivered in the language of truth; our play.'

(Applause. Vittoria comes backstage.)

VITTORIA: Some swear that we players must be true to our hearts. I say nothing of the kind. The stage is one big lie; it is what it is precisely because it has nothing of the truth upon it. It is all a marvelous deception, a hoax, a ruse to stimulate the fancies of the audience. They're not interested in sincerity - what could be more tedious than that? Give me the freedom to perjure reality, and I will give you a scintillating performance. I think the King liked me, don't you?

(Enter the Duke of Mantua.)

DUKE: Announcing His Serene Majesty, Charles, King of France.

(Enter King Charles IX of France, and his mother, Catherine de Medici. Ceremony.)

KING: Wonderful.

CATHERINE: His Serene Majesty was pleased with the performance.

44

DUKE: Your Most Serene Highness, the Gelosi is the first and certainly the best of the troupes of the commedia dell'arte. I am very proud to maintain the company in my employ.

(The King approaches Isabella.)

KING: Wonderful.

CATHERINE: His Serene Majesty was particularly taken with the skill and the finesse of Isabella. He was moved to tears by her simplicity. Formidable.

ISABELLA: Thank you, Your Serene Majesty.

CATHERINE: It is due to the impression that this young woman has made on His Serene Majesty that he is given to ask the Gelosi to visit his Court in Paris.

DUKE: On behalf of the Gelosi, I accept your most generous invitation, Your Serene Majesty.

CATHERINE: I will arrange safe passage. Come, Charles. They have agreed.

KING: Wonderful.

(Catherine and Charles exit. A stunned silence, then laughter, etc. Sylvia enters.)

SYLVIA: Everyone got what they need?

(Pause.)

SYLVIA: I'm the new maid. The other one got dropsy.

(Pause.)

SYLVIA: All right, don't all shout at once.

(She is about to leave.)

SYLVIA: If I may say so. Women on stage. Very good idea. Shake things up a bit.

VITTORIA: Girl. Wait a minute. What's her name?

SIMONE: Sylvia.

VITTORIA: Sylvia, come here.

(Sylvia crosses to Vittoria.)

SYLVIA: Yes, signorina?

VITTORIA: Are you a criminal, or a whore?

SYLVIA: Neither. My mother's a widow; my father was killed in the wars. I've scrubbed the Duke's floors since I was nine. I earn two coins a month and I get half a day off a year. That's it. Oh, I don't care for people and I can ride a horse tolerably well.

VITTORIA: I see. Well, you asked if there was anything I need, and there is. You.

SYLVIA: Me?

VITTORIA: I need a Lady-in-Waiting. I can't possibly go to the Court without one. You seem to be the only candidate for the position, so I will take you. I can take her, can't I, Vincenzo?

DUKE: Yes. Of course. Glad to be rid of her.

VITTORIA: Good. You're coming to Paris. Pack up your things.

SYLVIA: Yes, signorina.

(Sylvia exits.)

DUKE: I will make the arrangements. No expense will be spared. I need not stress how important it is that you make a good impression at the Court. Peachblossom, I will compose a letter of greeting to the French Court on your behalf. If you will come with me, I will give it to you.

VITTORIA: You can give it to my Lady-in-Waiting.

DUKE: I would rather give it to you.

VITTORIA: Just give it to my Lady-in-Waiting.

DUKE: What I have to give is for you and you alone, signorina.

VITTORIA: My Lady-in-Waiting will take care of it.

SIMONE: I think he wants to give it to you, signorina.

VITTORIA: I know perfectly well what he wants. But it is not what I want any more. A woman is not a courier. I do not march letters back and forth at the whim of anyone, signore.

DUKE: But the letter... is on your behalf...

VITTORIA: I need no letter, signore Duke. I can introduce myself at the French court perfectly well. And that is precisely what I intend to do. Independent of your ministrations.

DUKE: But...

VITTORIA: Is there anything else we can help you with, signore Duke?

DUKE: No.

VITTORIA: Very well. Then if you will excuse us.

DUKE: Of course.

(The Duke exits.)

ORAZIO: Vittoria.

VITTORIA: I expect that brought back all sorts of horrid memories, did it Orazio? Are you going to tell me I'm cruel? I shouldn't have broken your poor uncle's heart? Have you plucked up the courage to punch me on the nose, or curse me in public?

ORAZIO: I am still in love with you.

(Vittoria laughs.)

VITTORIA: You are priceless.

(She laughs on. Orazio exits.)

VITTORIA: *(to Isabella)* Incidentally, signora. In Paris the men have excellent taste. I think they may love me a little better there.

(She departs.)

GUILIO: We're going to the most powerful Court in Europe.

SIMONE: I'm going to eat till I pop.

GUILIO: We will play to kings and queens, princes and cardinals, nobles and duchesses. Cesco, can you believe it? After all these years.

FRANCESCO: We are nearly there. We are nearly in the belly of the beast.

ISABELLA: What do you mean by that?

FRANCESCO: Nothing, my love. Nothing at all.

PART 2: FRANCE

1. KIDNAP

(Night. The company is traveling by carriage to Paris. They are all squeezed in. Sound of the horses. Simone is asleep. Isabella is writing.)

GUILIO: Then we were attacked by a garrison of Turks. We were surrounded. We fought like maniacs. We killed fifty warriors. But there were too many of them. They captured twelve of us. They took us deep into the desert. There stood the prison. A monument to cruelty. We were incarcerated for six years. We endured the unendurable. One day, long after we thought we had passed the point of no return, the Turks released us into the desert with the words: 'It is finished.' There were three of us left. We had to walk back to Italy. By the time we reached Milan we were ghosts, not men. It was then that we found out the war had been over for three years.

VITTORIA: *(applauding)* I love war stories.

FRANCESCO: It's not a story, signorina.

VITTORIA: Embellish a little here, exaggerate a little there, and you've got your audience eating out of the palm of your hand. We should put it in the show.

FRANCESCO: Not everything in life is designed for amusement, signorina.

VITTORIA: I don't see any evidence to the contrary.

(The horses come to a halt.)

ORAZIO: We can't be in Paris already.

FRANCESCO: What's happening?

GUILIO: *(looking out)* I can't see. It's too dark.

(Sudden noise of swordplay.)

GUILIO: Oh shit.

ORAZIO: What is it? What's going on?

GUILIO: Two men wearing masks. I think they've killed our coachman.

(Vittoria screams.)

SIMONE: *(waking)* Roast pork!

ORAZIO: I pray.

FRANCESCO: Are you sure?

ISABELLA: Francesco, what's happening?

(Suddenly the horses start galloping. The carriage is taken at full speed, turning off in a new direction. Various expletives.)

GUILIO: All right! Everyone stay calm. We've been kidnapped.

(Vittoria screams.)

ORAZIO: I don't want to die, dear God, don't let me die!

FRANCESCO: Where are they taking us?

GUILIO: I can't see. It's too dark.

ORAZIO: In the name of God - who is doing this to us?

SYLVIA: The Huguenots, of course.

SIMONE: The who?

SYLVIA: The Huguenots. The Protestants.

ORAZIO: Mother of God!

VITTORIA: How do you know?

SYLVIA: They are the King's enemies. We are valuable to them. They'll hold us to ransom, kill us off one by one until the King meets their demands.

ORAZIO: I faint at the sight of blood.

(The coach comes to an abrupt halt.)

ORAZIO: Why have we stopped?

HUGUENOT: *(offstage)* Put down your weapons and come out.

VITTORIA: *(whispering)* Signori. You have slain many Turks in your day. Now it is your turn to slay the Huguenots.

SIMONE: I try not to do anything that will get me killed.

GUILIO: A sensible policy.

FRANCESCO: I agree.

HUGUENOT: *(offstage)* Come out by the count of ten. Or we kill you all. One. Two. Three.

(Etc. As he counts, chaos ensues. They all argue, nobody willing to be the one that steps outside, despite pushing and shoving.)

HUGUENOT: Nine...

(Pause. They wait.)

SIMONE: Sylvia!

FRANCESCO: *(covering Simone's mouth)* Shut up.

(A struggle. Simone desperate to speak, breaks free.)

SIMONE: She's not here.

(They discover that Sylvia has slipped out.)

FRANCESCO: What?

VITTORIA: My Lady-in-Waiting?

SIMONE: She's out there, with the Hooly-hoes.

ISABELLA: Huguenots.

SIMONE: She's going to be ravaged by the Hooly-hoes.

ISABELLA: Huguenots.

ORAZIO: Mother of God... Somebody stop this.

SIMONE: I'll rip them into little pieces. Come here, you Hooly-hoes, you demons and pigs. Let me plunge my hands into your chests and rip your hearts from their cavities, let me place the bloody still-beating organs into a pot, and boil them up with some carrots and a knuckle of ham, and then let me consume the entire dish in one gulp and wash it down with a sweet Belgian beer brewed by Dominicans.

VITTORIA: What's come over you all of a sudden?

SIMONE: I think I'm in love.

FRANCESCO: Will you shut up!

ISABELLA: Listen!

(They listen. From a distance, the sound of singing: a woman's voice.)

ISABELLA: She's singing.

SIMONE: Sylvia?

ISABELLA: She's singing.

(They gather around the carriage door, peeking out. Sylvia is singing a song.)

FRANCESCO: What song is that?

ISABELLA: I don't know.

(It ends. Applause, approval from the Huguenots outside.)

FRANCESCO: They're hypnotized.

SIMONE: Can you blame them? Encore!

(They shut him up.)

VITTORIA: Now she's dancing too.

(Sylvia is singing and dancing.)

ORAZIO: She possesses an uncommon degree of independence.

SIMONE: Please help me to marry her, Cesco, help me to marry her.

FRANCESCO: She's saving our lives.

GUILIO: Now what is she doing?

VITTORIA: She's getting very close to them.

SIMONE: She's a nightingale. A beautiful, innocent –

(A sudden gasp from all. Orazio faints.)

SIMONE: Shit.

GUILIO: She didn't.

FRANCESCO: She did.

(Sylvia arrives, wielding a knife spattered in blood.)

SYLVIA: It was them or us.

VITTORIA: I want a different Lady-in-Waiting.

SYLVIA: You're stuck with me. I'll take the place of the coachman. Hang on tight, I'd better give them the rein. This is Huguenot country.

(She exits. She comes back.)

SYLVIA: I only ask one thing for my troubles. I want to be in your play.

(She exits again. The coach lurches off.)

2. THE ARRIVAL

(Music. The company is dancing – the finale to their performance - at the Court of King Charles IX. Sylvia is prominent. The dance ends, the players leave. Charles enters the stage.)

KING: Wonderful. Beautiful. Play is very funny. King is very pleased. Terrible, horrible times. King is very scared...

(He begins to babble and cry. Catherine de Medici arrives.)

CATHERINE: His Serene Majesty declares the players welcome!

(She shepherds the King away. The company arrive backstage.)

SIMONE: Sylvia's debut was a triumph.

FRANCESCO: Gelosi, bravo.

GUILIO: I think they liked us.

ORAZIO: *(to Isabella)* Signora. You were magnificent – again.

SIMONE: Attention, everyone! Sylvia, I have prepared a little song to celebrate your debut.

(Simone sings.)

The moon is made of cheese
It even grows on trees

O won't you won't you please
Fly with me to the moon?

There's Edam, Roquefort, Brie
Asiago, Saint-Remy,
It's tasty and it's free
Fly with me to the moon.

O moon! In places you are hard! (Like Dutch cheese.)
O moon! In places you are soft! (Like French cheese.)

SYLVIA: Simone – stop.

SIMONE: I haven't finished.

SYLVIA: I get it.

SIMONE: Will you marry me?

SYLVIA: You don't want to know.

SIMONE: Please?

SYLVIA: No.

SIMONE: Why not?

SYLVIA: I don't believe in love.

FRANCESCO: Hear hear.

(Silence. Enter Catherine de Medici.)

CATHERINE: Mesdames, messieurs. You have won
the hearts of the Court. My sincere congratulations.
His Serene Majesty the King was moved to tears by
your performance.

58

(Catherine approaches Isabella.)

CATHERINE: You play like an angel, madame. A small token of my appreciation.

(She gives Isabella a necklace.)

ISABELLA: Thank you, Your Most Serene Highness.

CATHERINE: To whom should I present the wage for this afternoon's performance?

(Catherine hands over a pouch full of money to Francesco, who throws it to Guilio.)

FRANCESCO: We are your servants, Your Highness.

CATHERINE: And now, mesdames, messieurs, allow me to apologize for a certain incident that interrupted your journey here. These are unpredictable times. Our enemies are eager to surprise us. Nevertheless, rest assured that your security is guaranteed at this Court. *(To Francesco)* By the way, there is a moment in your play, monsieur, when you make a joke about the French. Do you remember?

FRANCESCO: 'I have made love with a thousand French women, each one more eager than the last.'

CATHERINE: Ah, no. I am thinking of something else... 'Let the French go to church on Sundays - I prefer women and wine.' Yes?

FRANCESCO: Is there anything the matter?

CATHERINE: Perhaps it could be changed a little. After all, we take mass five times a week. The notion of going on Sundays only, as your play implies, seems a little - Protestant.

(Awkward pause.)

FRANCESCO: We are players. We have no interest in matters of church.

CATHERINE: Perhaps not. But we all answer to His Illustrious Holiness Pope Gregory, do we not?

FRANCESCO: Not all of us.

GUILIO: Of course, Most Serene Highness. We will change the line in the play.

CATHERINE: I am delighted, messieurs, delighted. These are sensitive times; it pays to be cautious. Thank you so much. Please join us in the Great Hall for dancing and festivities. Fifty venison have been roasted and the King's orchestra is to play. We are honored to have you in Paris.

(Catherine exits.)

GUILIO: Cesco, we're at the Court of Charles IX. Your wife is the toast of Paris. Let's enjoy our good fortune.

SIMONE: Fifty roasted venison. I won't know what to do with myself.

GUILIO: Just keep making them laugh, Simone, and you can do whatever the hell you like.

(All exit, save Isabella and Francesco.)

ISABELLA: You don't believe in love.

FRANCESCO: There are more important things.

2. INTERRUPTION

VITTORIA: For once I agree with him.

(We are back in the Prologue.)

VITTORIA: Fame is more important than love. And we were famous.

FRANCESCO: What are you doing?

VITTORIA: This is precisely where our story should have ended.

FRANCESCO: What is she doing?

SYLVIA: She's interrupting. That's her style.

VITTORIA: Here, in the French court – we could have lived forever on the fat of the King's approval. We would have gone down in history as the best-known troupe in all of Europe.

GUILIO: We were rich. You can't deny it.

VITTORIA: I could have been a Countess, or a Marquise. I had a hundred admirers.

SIMONE: If I remember, Signora Andreini had all the admirers.

VITTORIA: *(to Simone)* You don't remember anything. You have the brain of a sausage.

SYLVIA: Leave him alone.

VITTORIA: You can shut up. If it weren't for your little crush on hotpants over there we'd never have gone through with his ridiculous plan.

SYLVIA: Have a little modesty, will you?

VITTORIA: You could have done with a little modesty yourself, before you kissed him on the mouth!

(Fracas.)

FRANCESCO: Enough! We have a story to tell.

(Silence. The Gelosi look sheepishly at the audience.)

FRANCESCO: *(to audience)* Signori. My apologies. It is 1572. We have been at the French Court for three months. The Gelosi have taken Paris by storm. They are eating out of the palms of our hands. But I am about to have an idea that will change...

GUILIO: Cesco.

(He points out Isabella, who is crying.)

FRANCESCO: Isabella.

ISABELLA: I remember each night. As if it were yesterday. I remember how cold it was.

FRANCESCO: That's not the story we are telling. That's just... two people.

ISABELLA: Of course. Continue with our story. The story of great men, and derring deeds.

FRANCESCO: I am about to have an idea that will change the theatre forever.

3. THE COUNCIL

(It is the middle of the night. The troupe enters, led by Francesco.)

FRANCESCO: Come quietly, please.

SIMONE: Why did you wake me up? Why did he wake us up?

ISABELLA: He wants to talk to us all.

SIMONE: Can't it wait until morning?

ISABELLA: Apparently not.

VITTORIA: Very intriguing.

SIMONE: What about breakfast? Since we're up we might as well have breakfast.

SYLVIA: It's too early for breakfast.

SIMONE: It's never too early for breakfast. Yesterday I had breakfast the night before, just to get a head start.

FRANCESCO: Signora, signorini, signori, welcome. Please make yourselves comfortable. If you are all ready, I declare this Council in session.

GUILIO: Council?

SIMONE: What's that?

ORAZIO: Why are we meeting in the middle of the night?

VITTORIA: For secrecy, I imagine.

FRANCESCO: That is correct, signorina. I ask you all to keep your voices down throughout the session. We don't want to arouse any suspicions. I've searched the theater in advance. We're alone.

GUILIO: What kind of Council?

FRANCESCO: This, signora, signorini, signori, is a Council of Retribution.

ISABELLA: Retribution?

FRANCESCO: No blood will be shed.

ISABELLA: Retribution for what?

FRANCESCO: For three months, now, we have pampered this Court with our comedies. We have given them laughter. We have given them verses. We have given them sweetness and light. And they have loved us in return, and showered us with reward. Why?

GUILIO: We are good at it.

FRANCESCO: True, and competence counts for something in this world. But there is another reason. My friends, we are cherished because we are frivolous. We are treasured because we are trivial. We are, in fact, the perfect distraction to this Court. While the King is laughing, he cannot be thinking.

SIMONE: My leg's gone to sleep.

GUILIO: Isn't that our job? To entertain?

FRANCESCO: This country is at war. Does that ever occur to you? This country is at war. There is an enemy out there. We almost fell foul of them ourselves. Every day, soldiers march on that enemy. Some will die. Some will be captured. Who knows? Maybe some poor bastards will be forgotten, just as we were, for six long years.

ORAZIO: But you were not men of France –

FRANCESCO: We answered to the same power. A power that holds Kings, Queens, Princes, Dukes in the palm of its hand. A power that sends men to war in its name, and abandons them.

(Beat.)

GUILIO: The church.

ISABELLA: Francesco, that's enough –

VITTORIA: You are playing with fire.

ORAZIO: Mother of God, I pray for forgiveness.

FRANCESCO: We were expendable. We were left for dead. Have you forgotten?

SIMONE: No.

FRANCESCO: And now look at us. Fat with success. Rich beyond our wildest dreams. Monkeys, dancing on the graves of men, while the audience applauds. We must remember who we are. We must remember who we are.

(Pause.)

66

FRANCESCO: I have written a play. It is a different kind of a play. It is not a play at all. It is a weapon. We will launch it without warning and it will smash into this Court, where it will explode in the hearts of all who are guilty.

ORAZIO: My uncle is not going to like this.

GUILIO: So this is what you've been sitting on.

FRANCESCO: Who is with me? Guilio, Simone, and I are three; who else is with me?

ISABELLA: I cannot declare for a man I do not trust.

FRANCESCO: What?

ISABELLA: All along I knew you were plotting. I asked you about it. You kept insisting it was nothing.

FRANCESCO: I couldn't reveal the nature of the operation. That would have jeopardized its integrity.

ISABELLA: It seems we have differing notions of integrity, Francesco.

VITTORIA: Nice.

FRANCESCO: Isabella – I don't think this is the moment to air our differences –

ISABELLA: This is exactly the moment. You have chosen this moment to declare yourself. I choose this moment to respond.

VITTORIA: Very nice.

ISABELLA: You wish to play at politics on the stage. What do you imagine will come of it, Francesco? Will you topple a monarch, or a pope? Will your retribution bring these poor soldiers you speak of any relief? Will all the miserable souls who rot in prisons today be miraculously set free? Can you give us a single precedent, a performance, or for that matter a sculpture, or a painting, or a poem, that has reversed the policies, the character, the decisions of a pontiff, a prince, a duke or a king? I think you have an elevated opinion of your influence, if you believe a play can turn the course of a war.

(Orazio applauds.)

VITTORIA: I am enjoying this enormously.

ISABELLA: Your literary enterprise has been a secret until now, but mine has not. As you well know, I have been writing my own play. It is entitled *The Madness of Isabella*. It is a poetic meditation on the agonies of falling in love. I wish to touch hearts, not to explode them. I hereby submit my play as an alternative to my husband's folly.

VITTORIA: This gets better and better.

FRANCESCO: It seems we are faced with a choice. On the one hand, my play; on the other, my wife's. Make your positions known. Our contract states that we may decide internal conflicts by means of the majority. Guilio, Simone and I dwell in one camp. My wife dwells in another. Which is it for you?

ORAZIO: I declare for your wife, signore. Poetry is the whispering of the gods in the orchards of the spheres -

FRANCESCO: Two for Isabella. Signorina?

VITTORIA: You're both wrong, of course. You make it so complicated and exhausting. I refuse to walk the stage in the shadow of an idea. It would dim my radiance. Thank God, this whole business is simple for me. To be celebrated; that is all I seek, and what better place to seek it than the stage? Now, if we are ejected from Paris I shall not find myself on the stage, and if not on the stage, I shall not be as celebrated. Ergo: I declare for your wife, signore.

FRANCESCO: Three for Isabella, and three for me. That leaves Sylvia as the casting vote.

SYLVIA: If the signora will forgive me, I choose for the signore. I find his position more persuasive. Poetry has its charms, but I don't think it's a very faithful cousin to reality. The way people talk on the stage is nothing like the way they talk in life; and the way that they fall in love is perfectly silly.

ISABELLA: I do not say that love is easy.

SYLVIA: I'm not suggesting that you do, signora, you're far too intelligent for that. But I have an aversion to sentiment in any disguise. What the world needs is something altogether different. I'm quite certain that your husband's play won't compare to yours when it comes to literature: but I believe, in the end, that we're better off with one drop of anger than a flood of fine writing.

FRANCESCO: Four for me, three for Isabella. The decision is made.

VITTORIA: Funny how that worked out.

FRANCESCO: We will rehearse in secret. Then, presto! We're going to wipe those smiles off their faces. This Council is adjourned.

GUILIO: Cesco.

FRANCESCO: What is it?

GUILIO: I declare for your wife.

FRANCESCO: What?

GUILIO: I don't agree with her either, but at least she hasn't gone mad.

FRANCESCO: Are you serious?

GUILIO: A man watches a play. Then he goes home. That's it. Whether he screws his wife or invades Poland, it makes no difference to me. As long as he puts money in the hat I can stand up there the next night and do it again. I can eat good food and drink good wine and sleep on a soft pillow and maybe every now and then a woman flutters her eyes at me. That's enough, isn't it, Cesco? That's our life now. There's nothing wrong with it. We've come too far to throw it all away.

FRANCESCO: Guilio. After all we've been through –

GUILIO: No. I don't bear a grudge any more, Cesco. It's just history.

FRANCESCO: You like being rich and successful.

GUILIO: Is that a crime?

FRANCESCO: Guilio. We're the Gelosi, remember? Six years we rotted.

GUILIO: But thirty years we could flourish.

FRANCESCO: You're a deserter.

GUILIO: I desert madness in favor of sanity.

VITTORIA: Four to three, Isabella.

GUILIO: Hey.

SIMONE: What?

GUILIO: Quit leaving me hung out to dry, will you?

SIMONE: Erm. Cesco.

FRANCESCO: What do you want?

SIMONE: I think I might. Also. Sort of. Change my.

GUILIO: Say it, numbskull.

SIMONE: I declare for your wife.

VITTORIA: Five to two, ouch.

SIMONE: I think you have treated her badly. And I think she deserves better.

ISABELLA: Simone -

FRANCESCO: What the hell has that got to do with anything?

SIMONE: I don't know. But I declare for her anyway.

FRANCESCO: She deserves better? Where are your guts, you piece of shit? I ought to carve my name on your balls, you moron -

(Francesco draws his sword.)

GUILIO: Leave him alone.

FRANCESCO: Is there a single man here who is loyal to me?

VITTORIA: Not a man, no.

FRANCESCO: I'll take you all on.

GUILIO: Put that thing down, for the last time.

ISABELLA: Francesco, stop it!

SYLVIA: Someone's coming!

FRANCESCO: Quick. Hide. If they find us in Council, they'll know we're up to something.

SIMONE: But we're not up to anything.

FRANCESCO: They don't know that. Hide. Everyone, hide.

(They all hide. The King enters, pursued by Catherine de Medici.)

CATHERINE: Come back to bed, my darling boy, don't cry.

KING: Leave me alone, mummy.

CATHERINE: Charles – I just want to talk to you –

KING: No!

CATHERINE: You're upset, I know.

KING: Yes I am upset. It is a horrible idea, I will not do it. I have a conscience.

CATHERINE: But it is not your idea, Charles. It is God's idea. His Most Supreme Illustrious Holiness Pope Gregory has sent word. He expresses his complete approval. Your conscience has nothing to do with it.

KING: Gregory?

CATHERINE: He applauds any measure aimed at the Huguenots. No matter how severe. Now sign the order, darling boy.

KING: Applauds... Where are the players?

CATHERINE: Never mind the players.

KING: Where are the players, I say?

CATHERINE: It's the middle of the night, Charles. I am sure they are in and out of one another's beds.

KING: I like the players. I like to laugh.

73

CATHERINE: Yes, Charles, and that is why the players are here. Now sign the order. Or else one day a nasty Huguenot will kill you first.

KING: I want to see a play.

CATHERINE: You can't see a play now.

KING: I'm the King, I can see a play when I want.

CATHERINE: Forget about the players, will you? They don't matter.

KING: They matter to me.

CATHERINE: Of course they matter to you, darling. I mean that they don't matter to God.

KING: If I didn't have the players I'd go mad.

CATHERINE: Please stop talking about the players.

KING: 'Look at me. I'm Pantalone. Ooh! Pantalone, I am a chaste maid, do not pinch my bottom! Ooh!'

CATHERINE: Damn the players, Charles! I wish those Satanists had killed them!

KING: What?

CATHERINE: What?

KING: What did you just say?

(Pause.)

KING: Did you try to kill the players, mummy?

74

CATHERINE: I arranged for them to be captured by the Huguenots.

KING: Mummy?

CATHERINE: It was a political decision, Charles.

KING: But why?

CATHERINE: Because then we could have killed a number of Huguenots with impunity. In retaliation.

KING: You wanted the players to be killed?

CATHERINE: I don't care about the players one way or the other. I was just trying to find good reason for a bloodbath. Look, it doesn't matter, with Gregory's approval we are authorized to strike first. We don't need reasons any more. Now will you please sign the order, Charles, before I lose my temper?

KING: I love the players.

CATHERINE: Perhaps the players have outstayed their welcome in Paris.

KING: No.

CATHERINE: The Court has become licentious since their arrival. Their dismissal would remind us all of the need for piety. Rome would be very satisfied.

KING: No.

CATHERINE: Was it not His Illustrious Holiness Gregory himself who wrote "we must eliminate the terrible virus of those abominable and pernicious comedies"? Let the players be expelled tomorrow.

KING: No, no, no! I don't want the players to leave.

CATHERINE: You heard the words of Pope Gregory, Charles.

KING: Please, please, please.

CATHERINE: Then sign the order, Charles. Let the Huguenots die and the players shall stay. I shall vouch for them.

KING: You promise?

CATHERINE: I promise.

KING: What would I have in my head if the players didn't fill it up with nonsense?

CATHERINE: Sign the order, Charles.

KING: I have no ink.

(Catherine jabs the quill into Charles's arm.)

KING: Ahhh!

CATHERINE: Royal ink.

KING: In the name of His Most Supreme Illustrious Holiness, Pope Gregory XIII, I sign this order. Let the blood be on his hands.

(He signs.)

CATHERINE: In five days our men will be ready. There will be rivers of blood in the streets of Paris.

(She leaves, with the order.)

KING: Mummy. Mummy, kiss it better…

(He runs after her. The Gelosi emerge from hiding.)

FRANCESCO: Who is with me now?

<u>INTERMISSION</u>

5. HUNCHBACKS

(An expectant hum from the audience. The King comes on stage.)

KING: And now, the Italian Comedians.

(Applause. The King takes his seat.)

(First Hunchback enters (Francesco). All Hunchbacks are dressed identically, all wear Pulcinella-inspired masks. At certain moments they are prone to gleeful giggling, part-children, part-sadists.)

FIRST HUNCHBACK: 'Welcome All and Welcome Friends / Peace Gelosi To You Sends / I Am Here To You Advise / We For You Have Big Surprise / Play Tonight Will Be Unique / Hope Your Interest We Will Pique / Now Sit Back Enjoy The Fun / Here Begin Our Play Scene One. *(He steps forward.)* I Present You Little Game / I Am One You Know By Name / I Am One You Know, My Friends / Can You Name Me By The End? / From My Missions Try Surmise / Whether You Me Recognize / Listen What I Say And Be / Guess My True Identity.'

(Three hunchbacks step forward - the Hunchback Chorus of Simone, Sylvia, Guilio.)

FIRST HUNCHBACK: 'Here Come Men To Start Our Play / Listen What I Be And Say.'

HUNCHBACK SOLDIERS: 'We are Soldiers. We are Poor.'

FIRST HUNCHBACK: 'If You Poor You go to War.'

HUNCHBACK CHORUS: 'What If We Go War Get Killed?'

FIRST HUNCHBACK: 'Long As My Blood Not Be Spilled.'

(The Hunchback Chorus go to war and get repeatedly killed.)

FIRST HUNCHBACK: 'War Is Not To Me Inviting / I Don't Mind If They Die Fighting / They Want Win For Me Then Let Them / If They Die I Soon Forget Them.'

(The Hunchback Chorus are dead.)

FIRST HUNCHBACK: 'End of Scene. In Peace They Rest. / Which Of You Has My Name Guessed?'

HUNCHBACK CHORUS: *(reviving)* ' Second Scene. Three Have Survived. / But In Prison Have Arrived. / We In Prison, Save Us Please. / We Fought With Your Enemies / We Gave Up Our Freedom For You / Rescue Us We Now Implore You.'

FIRST HUNCHBACK: 'War Has Ended, Happily / I Sit Home In Luxury / Eat My Favorite Dinner (Monkfish) / Pronounce Mission Well Accomplished.'

HUNCHBACK CHORUS: 'We Forsaken, We Forgotten / We In Turkish Jail Have Rotten.'

FIRST HUNCHBACK: 'End Scene Two. Remember Me / I Will Return After Scene Three.'

HUNCHBACK CHORUS: 'We Survive the War, Agree / Players Is What We Shall Be / Players Poor We Play for Bread / Better (Just) than Being Dead.'

(A Hunchback Woman arrives – Vittoria.)

HUNCHBACK WOMAN: 'I Sweet Woman I Decide / I join Players Side by Side.'

HUNCHBACK CHORUS: 'Woman Play And Many Come / See How Play Is Naughty Fun.'

(Hunchback Woman is now part of the Chorus. Enter a Hunchback Duke – Isabella.)

HUNCHBACK DUKE: 'I am Duke I Come See Players / Look Like Answer to My Prayers / They are Making Plenty Splash / This Be Easy Way Make Cash / Come here Players!'

HUNCHBACK CHORUS: 'Yes Signore?'

HUNCHBACK DUKE: 'You Want Money? I Give More.'

HUNCHBACK CHORUS: 'Players Happy! All Excited! / Specially When To King Invited!'

(The Hunchback King enters – Orazio.)

HUNCHBACK KING: 'Welcome Players to Fancy Land / I am King Please Shake My Hand.'

HUNCHBACK CHORUS: 'Hello King We Shake You Gladly / We Desire To Please You Madly.'

(They fondle him.)

HUNCHBACK KING: 'Players Naughty! Players Funny! / Players Watch Out For My Mummy.'

(Hunchback Queen Mother – Isabella - enters.)

HUNCHBACK QUEEN MOTHER: 'I Agree Play Is Well Acted / But My Son Be Not Distracted / Out The Palace Very Urgent / City Full Of Foul Insurgents / Every Day The Threat It Grows / From the Dreaded Hooly-hoes.'

ALL: 'Hooly-hoes are Evil, Bad.'

HUNCHBACK KING: 'Hooly-hoes Make Mummy Mad.'

HUNCHBACK QUEEN MOTHER: 'Hooly-hoes Are Satan Spawn / We Should Kill Them All By Dawn.'

(Hunchback Chorus makes wild killing gestures.)

HUNCHBACK KING: 'Wait! Before This Grisly End / First I Ask My Bestest Friend / Let My Bestest Friend Advise Me / Lest The Lord God Should Despise Me.'

FIRST HUNCHBACK: *(returning)* 'End Scene Three. Now I Return / Soon My Name You Will All Learn / If Anyone Remain Unsure / Await The Climax of Scene Four.'

(All Hunchbacks set up for Scene 4 – Chorus, including Hunchback Queen Mother, at rear, Hunchback King DSL, First Hunchback DSR.)

HUNCHBACK KING: 'Friend O Friend To You I Come / When The Day Is Over Done / When The

Hour Of Prayer Is Here / Yours The Voice I Seek To Hear / Over Us You Do Preside / And Our Fates You Help Decide / What Am I To Do With Those / Accursed Loathsome Hooly-Hoes?'

FIRST HUNCHBACK: 'Friend I Glad To Hear Your Query / Though You Far I Feel You Near Me / Not So Crazy After All / I So Big and You So Small / I In Charge of Everything / Even I in Charge of King / I Gods Messenger on Earth / You Are Mine Till Death from Birth / If I Say Jump You Jump For Me / If I Say Kill Then You Agree / If You Catholic (Which You Must Be) / God Insist You Really Trust Me / You're Either With Me Or You're Not / And If You're Not, In Hell You'll Rot.'

(Under the next part of First Hunchback's speech, the other Hunchbacks join in a 'whispering chorus', building slowly to crescendo.)

FIRST HUNCHBACK: 'Thus I Give You My Decree / Make Sure It Is Done For Me / I Decree That Everyone / Get Up Off Their Lazy Bum / Grab a Sword and Go Outside / And Skin a Hooly-hoe Alive / Chop His Dick Off Or Her Tits / Chop Them Into Little Bits / Roast Their Hearts and Boil Their Heads / And Stab Their Children in Their Beds / Now Not Time For Peace Goodwill / Now Is Time to Murder-Kill / Dispatch the Hooly-Hoes to Hell / Decimate the Infidel / Kill and Kill Tis My Decree / Kill Till All Of Us Be Free / This How Holy War It Works / Whether Hooly -hoes or Turks / If Not Catholics All the Same / And Holy War My Favorite Game!'

(Silence. The last part of text is First Hunchback only.)

FIRST HUNCHBACK: 'Have You Guessed Yet Who I Be? / Champion of Liberty / Everyone Abandon Hope / I Am Gregory Your Pope.'

(Complete silence. Slowly, laughter from the King.)

KING: Funny!

(Catherine de Medici marches onto the stage. She takes the mask from Francesco's face.)

CATHERINE: If this man is a Huguenot, let him say it.

FRANCESCO: I am just a player.

CATHERINE: He commits sacrilege against our Church.

FRANCESCO: I do not believe in your Church.

GUILIO: *(takes off his mask)* Nor I.

SIMONE: *(takes off his mask)* Nor I.

CATHERINE: Then messieurs: prepare to join your friends in Hell.

(Crowd noises, roaring. We are outside the palace. Spotlight on Catherine, who reads from the order.)

CATHERINE: By order of His Serene Majesty King Charles IX of France, on this day of St Bartholemew, 24 August, 1572 the Year of Our Lord. Let every Huguenot in Paris, man, woman, or child, be brought before the Palace and hanged, in the name of the Father, the Son, the Blessed Virgin and the Holy Church of our Faith. These men shall be the first.

(An almighty roar. Francesco, Guilio and Simone are led to the gallows by a mysterious Executioner. A rope is placed around their necks. Drums, roar of crowd.)

CATHERINE: These are the players that have tarnished the Court of our King with their depravity. They are sent by the Huguenots, vassals of the anti-Christ, to sow lust in our hearts. They are demons. Let them hang.

(Crowd roars. The Executioner prepares to kill them. Suddenly reveals herself to be Sylvia. Wielding her knife, she fights off several guards, cuts down the three men from the gallows.)

SYLVIA: Run!

(Mayhem. The players escape.)

PART 3: ITALY

1. EXILE

(The company arrives at the gates of Mantua.)

FRANCESCO: Citizens of Mantua!

VOICE: *(offstage)* Who goes there?

FRANCESCO: We are the company Gelosi. We have fled from the Court of Charles IX. We have come home to our patron. Let us in.

VOICE: *(offstage)* The Gelosi are not welcome in Mantua.

FRANCESCO: The Duke of Mantua is our patron.

VOICE: *(offstage)* The Gelosi are not welcome in Mantua.

FRANCESCO: You've made a mistake. We are the Gelosi, the players. The Duke's players.

VOICE: *(offstage)* The Gelosi are not welcome in Mantua.

FRANCESCO: Hey. Listen. It's the middle of the night. We need shelter. There are women here.

VOICE: *(offstage)* The gates of Mantua are closed to the Gelosi.

FRANCESCO: Let us in, you bastard, or I'll carve my name –

GUILIO: That's enough, Cesco.

FRANCESCO: I want to speak to the Duke. I was nearly killed.

SYLVIA: The Duke cannot let us in. He fears reprisals from the Pope, or the French.

SIMONE: But I'm hungry. I didn't eat for three days.

FRANCESCO: What kind of miserable shit leaves his own theater company starving at the gates of his city?

ORAZIO: There's no need to be rude about my uncle.

FRANCESCO: You shut your face.

ISABELLA: Francesco, calm down.

FRANCESCO: I will not calm down. We have to talk to the Duke. We'll bribe our way in. Guilio, give me some money.

GUILIO: We haven't got any money.

FRANCESCO: What do you mean we haven't got any money?

GUILIO: We haven't got any money.

FRANCESCO: What about the cash box?

GUILIO: Catherine is probably emptying it right now.

FRANCESCO: You didn't bring it with you?

GUILIO: It must have slipped my mind. When I was standing on the gallows.

SIMONE: No money?

FRANCESCO: We had thousands of coins. We need that money.

GUILIO: Now he wants his money. Did you like being rich after all?

SIMONE: No more pies.

FRANCESCO: Isabella, we'll have to sell your jewelry.

ISABELLA: I don't have my jewelry.

FRANCESCO: You don't have your -? Why not?

ISABELLA: Because we barely escaped with our lives, Francesco.

FRANCESCO: Am I surrounded by imbeciles?

GUILIO: Quit blaming everyone, will you? This is your fault.

FRANCESCO: My fault?

GUILIO: Yes, your fault. I knew it would end in disaster. I should never have gone along with it.

SIMONE: I second that.

ORAZIO: Neither should I.

ISABELLA: It was ill-judged, Francesco.

FRANCESCO: But you did go along with it. All of you.

GUILIO: I'll regret it forever.

SIMONE: Me too.

ORAZIO: And I.

GUILIO: We're pariahs now. Wherever we go we'll be pariahs. You have ruined our future.

FRANCESCO: Not one of you has the courage of your convictions.

GUILIO: Conviction is one thing. Lunacy is another.

FRANCESCO: Are you calling me a lunatic?

GUILIO: Yes.

FRANCESCO: You know where I'll carve my name.

GUILIO: How about I carve my knuckles on your face?

VITTORIA: You're all lunatics, all of you. We were at the Court of a King. A King. We've thrown away a glorious future. For what? For what? For the sake of a stupid play.

SYLVIA: I will never regret it. It was the bravest thing that any of us have ever done.

VITTORIA: You would say that.

SYLVIA: What's that supposed to mean?

VITTORIA: You know exactly what it's supposed to mean.

FRANCESCO: All right, that's enough.

SIMONE: Leave her alone, will you?

VITTORIA: How charming. Two knights in shining armor. Which one will sweep her off her feet, I wonder?

SYLVIA: I'd like to scratch your eyes out.

VITTORIA: Why? Are you afraid they've seen something?

(Sylvia lunges at Vittoria. A huge fracas.)

ISABELLA: Stop it. All of you, stop it. We are not animals.

(Pause.)

ISABELLA: So we have lost our reputation, is that a reason to tear each other to pieces? My husband made a mistake, you did, Francesco, but I am not going to punish you for it, and nor should anyone else. We are down on our luck, so be it. If we cannot play in the cities, we can play in the country. We can travel to the provinces. We can perform *The Madness of Isabella* and we can regain our following, little by little. We can survive.

VITTORIA: How enticing.

ISABELLA: If you don't like it, signorina, then come up with an alternative.

(Pause.)

ISABELLA: Now it is time to sleep. We can talk more in the morning.

(The company disperse, grumbling.)

SIMONE: *(lying down)* It's cold.

ORAZIO: I can't possibly lie down here.

SIMONE: You can't sleep standing up. Unless you're a horse.

VITTORIA: Sylvia, get me a blanket.

SYLVIA: Get it yourself.

SIMONE: Sylvia, there's a place for you next to me.

SYLVIA: No thanks.

(The company settle down next to each other to sleep.)

SIMONE: This reminds me of prison.

GUILIO: Fond memories.

(Silence falls.)

GUILIO: Simone?

SIMONE: What?

GUILIO: Move over, will you? I need more room.

SIMONE: All right.

2. ONE LAST CHANCE

(Morning. The company, minus Vittoria, are asleep. Sylvia and Francesco are sitting apart, speaking privately.)

FRANCESCO: I never had the chance to say thanks. For saving our lives.

SYLVIA: No bother.

(Pause.)

FRANCESCO: Everyone hates me.

SYLVIA: It will pass.

FRANCESCO: Guilio hates me.

SYLVIA: It will pass.

(Francesco chuckles.)

FRANCESCO: Her face.

SYLVIA: Catherine?

FRANCESCO: I'll never forget it. We skewered her.

SYLVIA: We did.

(Pause.)

FRANCESCO: I don't know what we're going to do.

SYLVIA: Tour the provinces, by the look of things.

FRANCESCO: Not much of a life, after what we've been used to.

SYLVIA: I know.

FRANCESCO: Where did you learn to look after yourself?

SYLVIA: When you're a maid, you scrub the floor all day, your ass is pointing in the air – you get a lot of unwanted attention, if you know what I mean. Dukes and Cardinals are the worst – they don't even bother to ask. If you don't want to surrender, you have to learn how to fight. With your hands.

FRANCESCO: You don't believe in love.

SYLVIA: Not a bit.

(He kisses her. Vittoria enters, unseen.)

SIMONE: *(with a start)* Ah!

(Francesco and Sylvia move away from each other.)

GUILIO: What is it?

SIMONE: I was about to be hanged.

ORAZIO: *(getting up suddenly)* Where's Vittoria?

VITTORIA: Good morning.

ORAZIO: Vittoria. I was worried about you. Where have you been?

VITTORIA: Oh, I couldn't bear the horrible ground for a whole night. I just had to find myself somewhere comfortable to sleep. A nice bed, with fresh linen. A balcony with a view of the hills. Yes, your uncle was very accommodating.

ORAZIO: Uncle?

VITTORIA: Yes, you're going to be very pleased with me. I have pacified our patron. He was very angry, oh, he was spitting mad, he never wanted to see us again. We dishonored the Court – we jeopardized relations – we were very bad players. But after a little pleading, cajoling, a little feminine soothing, he came around. And I do believe he has a proposition for us. Signora, you asked for an alternative: here it comes.

(The Duke of Mantua enters.)

DUKE: Gelosi.

ORAZIO: Uncle.

ISABELLA: Allow me to apologize, signore Duke, on behalf of the Gelosi, for our improper conduct in Paris.

DUKE: I cannot understand what possessed you, to take aim at the King, and Gregory.

ISABELLA: A dose of hubris, signore, which we deeply regret.

DUKE: That's putting it mildly. However, as I am reminded, a little mischief is only to be expected from a troupe of players. That is part of the charm of the theater, is it not? Very well. I accept your apology. We are still under contract, after all, and commerce brooks no patience with feelings. To business. The Grand Duke of Florence is getting married next month. I will be attending his wedding, and I wish to offer him a performance by the Gelosi as a gift. It will be an important engagement. Florence is dear to my heart. You will have the chance to mend your reputation. Assuming you are on your best behavior.

ISABELLA: Signore. We are most grateful for your offer. We won't let you down. No more politics, we promise.

DUKE: Excellent. It will be mutually beneficent. I will send word to Florence. I am very glad to have you back, Gelosi!

(He leaves.)

SIMONE: That's good, isn't it?

GUILIO: Thank God for that.

ORAZIO: I knew uncle would assist us in our plight.

VITTORIA: A perfect alternative, don't you think, signora? Rather the Grand Duke of Florence than an eternity in the provinces.

ISABELLA: Yes. Thank you, signorina. Gelosi. We will prepare *The Madness of Isabella* for Florence. Is everyone ready? Shall we rehearse?

(The Duke returns.)

DUKE: Oh – one small thing. There is a condition to the offer. It is a matter of the choice of play.

ISABELLA: The Gelosi provides its own material, signore.

DUKE: Yes, I expect nothing less, of course.

ISABELLA: Then your condition is met.

DUKE: Not exactly. On this occasion I choose Signorina Piissimi to be the author of your play. Yes.

ISABELLA: I did not know that the signorina wrote plays.

VITTORIA: Oh – didn't I tell you? I must have forgotten.

DUKE: She's very accomplished. I have read many of her plays. In the past. Before you knew her.

ISABELLA: Signore Duke, with the greatest respect, you cannot dictate -

DUKE: Clause 66. The patron has the final authority over all presentations.

ISABELLA: Signore, would you leave us to confer for a moment?

DUKE: Of course, of course.

(He retires.)

ISABELLA: I must object to the condition.

VITTORIA: I knew it.

ISABELLA: This is a fraudulent bid to usurp me –

VITTORIA: The signora is envious, pure and simple.

ISABELLA: She has corrupted our patron with her wiles -

VITTORIA: Let the signora remember that we are under contract.

ISABELLA: Then let us break the contract and go our own way.

VITTORIA: To the provinces?

ISABELLA: I can't stand it, I can't stand it. We must perform my play.

VITTORIA: We seem to be facing a choice. On the one hand, the signora's play, no contract, no patron, and the provinces: sleeping out in the rain, nothing to eat, bugs crawling up our legs, a few coins between us, anonymity. On the other hand, my play, full patronage, and the wedding of the Grand Duke of Florence: good food, soft beds, a real wage, our reputation repaired, a promising future. Now who declares for the signora?

(Pause. Isabella runs off.)

FRANCESCO: Isabella…

VITTORIA: That's settled, then. Vincenzo!

(The Duke returns.)

VITTORIA: The Gelosi are delighted to accept your condition.

DUKE: A wise decision. Peachblossom.

(He leaves.)

VITTORIA: Orazio, would you be a good boy and fetch parchment and quill? Most of my play is in my head – you'll just have to write it down for me.

ORAZIO: Yes, signorina.

VITTORIA: Don't worry, signori, there are parts for you all, and a terribly gripping story. Don't take anything personally; it's all just a fiction, you know. It's full of the most unbearable lies.

3. THE MADNESS OF ISABELLA

(At the wedding of the Grand Duke of Florence. Vittoria's play.)

VITTORIA: *'O misery. O dread, O woe. O bitter, galling, anguish. O pain. O ache. O soreness, throbbing, burning, pestitudinal hurtness. Must a woman break another woman's heart? Must it fall to me, Princess of All that is Lovely, to let fall the anvil? Hush, soft, mum, mute; here comes the unsuspecting lady.'*

(Enter Ermintrude, i.e. Isabella.)

ISABELLA: *'Have you seen my husband, Vittoria?'*

VITTORIA: *(prompting)* 'O princess.'

ISABELLA: *'Have you seen my husband, Vittoria, O princess?'*

VITTORIA: *'My dear Ermintrude, you have long been like an older sister to me; older, more severe, with a thicker neck. You have helped me in hundreds of ways; sewing my dresses and brushing out my hair and delivering messages from handsome strangers. Now I fear I must repay you with the bitterest of news. O misery. O dread, O woe. O bitter, galling-'*

ISABELLA: *'What is your news, Vittoria, O Princess?'*

VITTORIA: *'Come with me, my matronly friend, to my Palace of Beauty, where I must show you a sight to chill your marrow.'*

(They exit. Arlecchino enters.)

ARLECCHINO (SIMONE): *'The great Palace of Beauty. Our Princess Vittoria lives here, and rules over us all. She is good, she is kind, she is truly ben-elephant.'*

VITTORIA: *(off, prompting)* 'Benevolent.'

ARLECCHINO (SIMONE): *I said, ben-elephant. 'It is my job to sweep the floors every day; and if I'm lucky, catch a glimpse of Sylvia, my love, the scullery-maid. But I have not seen her much recently – where can she be?'*

(Enter Leandro and Pantalone.)

PANTALONE (GUILIO) / LEANDRO (ORAZIO): *'Friend, which way to the Palace of Beauty?'*

ARLECCHINO (SIMONE): *'Right here.'*

PANTALONE (GUILIO): *'I have come from fifty miles to ask for the hand of the Princess in marriage.'*

LEANDRO (ORAZIO): *'And I have come from one hundred miles to ask for the hand of the Princess in marriage.'*

PANTALONE (GUILIO): *'In my opinion, the Princess is the most splendid woman in the world.'*

LEANDRO (ORAZIO): *'In my opinion, the Princess is the most magnificent woman in the world.'*

PANTALONE (GUILIO): *'She is modest.'*

LEANDRO (ORAZIO): *'She is virtuous.'*

PANTALONE (GUILIO): *'She is wise.'*

LEANDRO (ORAZIO): *'She is pure.'*

PANTALONE (LEANDRO): *'Her lips are red.'*

LEANDRO (ORAZIO): *'Her cheeks are white.'*

PANTALONE (GUILIO): *'Her hands are soft.'*

LEANDRO (ORAZIO): *'Her bosoms sheer.'*

PANTALONE (GUILIO): *'I am frenzied.'*

LEANDRO (ORAZIO): *'I'm possessed.'*

PANTALONE (GUILIO): *'I must have her.'*

LEANDRO (ORAZIO): *'I must have her first.'*

PANTALONE (GUILIO) / LEANDRO (ORAZIO): *'Or I would rather die.'*

(Vittoria and Isabella enter. The two men prostrate themselves.)

PANTALONE (GUILIO) / LEANDRO (ORAZIO): *'O Princess...'*

VITTORIA: *'I will hear your suits later, signori.'*

PANTALONE (GUILIO) / LEANDRO (ORAZIO): *'Unless we are answered now, we will kill ourselves.'*

VITTORIA: *'Then kill yourselves you must, for I have tragic business in hand, and I will not be diverted from my course.'*

PANTALONE (GUILIO) / LEANDRO (ORAZIO): *'We have no choice.'*

(They kill themselves abruptly.)

VITTORIA: *'Night is falling. Let us conceal here, older friend, and extinguish our lamp - for they meet here in the dark. Soon we will soon see the awful truth - soon.'*

(They hide.)

ARLECCHINO (SIMONE): *'It is night. It is pitch dark. I can't see a thing. Might as well fall asleep.'*

(He falls asleep. Enter Capitano Spavento – Francesco - and Sylvia.)

CAPITANO (FRANCESCO): *'I have made love to ten thousand women, but not one has inspired me as you do, wench.'*

SYLVIA: *'But sire, you are married.'*

CAPITANO (FRANCESCO): *'Pah! There is nothing to marriage at all. It is a convenience. Why, if my wife had not had a good voice and passable figure and helped me to achieve things that I could never have done without her, I would never have married her in the first place!'*

SYLVIA: *'O Capitano. Take me, I beg you.'*

CAPITANO (FRANCESCO): *'Pull up your skirt, wench, and let me explore the flavors of the Orient.'*

SYLVIA: *'It is true I have been a side-dish for many a man.'*

CAPITANO (FRANCESCO): *'Where are you? It is so dark I cannot see.'*

SYLVIA: *'Over here.'*

(Accidentally, the Capitano gets hold of Arlecchino.)

ARLECCHINO (SIMONE): *'Good morning.'*

CAPITANO (FRANCESCO): *'Come along, Sylvia. Open wide.'*

ARLECCHINO (SIMONE): *'Is it time for breakfast?'*

SYLVIA: *'I can't feel anything, Capitano.'*

CAPITANO (FRANCESCO): *'Just bend over a little and you will soon feel my authority.'*

ARLECCHINO (SIMONE): *'Breakfast sausage.'*

SYLVIA: *'Still nothing, Capitano. I am so lonely.'*

CAPITANO (FRANCESCO): *'How's THAT?'*

ARLECCHINO: *'OOOOAAAWWW! Spicy sausage.'*

(Vittoria emerges with the lamp.)

VITTORIA: *'Caught red-handed, you lecherous Spaniard.'*

CAPITANO (FRANCESCO): *'Arlecchino? What are you doing here? Take that, you monstrous pervert.'*

(The Capitano wallops Arlecchino.)

SYLVIA: *'Oh don't hurt the pathetic fool. It's not his fault: I am guilty. The Capitano and I are lovers and have been for some time. Nobody knew except you, O wise and munificent Princess, for nothing escapes your divine perceptions.'*

VITTORIA: *'Kneel before me, sinners.'*

(Capitano and Sylvia kneel.)

VITTORIA: *'Capitano Spaventi; I have here your wife Ermintrude. She has seen your evil and now you must face her.'*

(Isabella is frozen.)

VITTORIA: *'Come forward, older woman, and face your adulterous husband.'*

(Pause.)

VITTORIA: *(prompting)* 'O you heartless. You heartless swine.'

(Pause.)

VITTORIA: *'As I suspected. Her heart is broke. O misery. O dread, O woe. But wait, what's this? A magic wand. My friends, this tale is but a parable. It did not happen at all.'*

(She waves a magic wand. Everyone except Ermintrude/ Isabella, including Pantalone & Leandro, who are revived, cheers up.)

CAPITANO (FRANCESCO): *'I just had the strangest dream.'*

ALL: *(save Isabella) So did we.*

VITTORIA: *'This is but a warning to husbands, no more / Our Captain is honest and true / For marriage is wonderful, magical, sure / And so it can be for you.'*

(The play is about to end, when Isabella - no longer even attempting to be in the play - cries, a low, long cry. Pause.)

VITTORIA: *'This is but a warning to husbands, no more-'*

ISABELLA: What is a man? A man is a ghost. He lives on in the house of love, long after he has died; he haunts every corner of a woman's heart. Sometimes he won't even admit that he is dead; with soothing words, he deceives her into thinking that he is still flesh and blood. This is the worst of all – to believe in a man who has already gone.

VITTORIA: *'This is but a warning to husbands, no more-'*

ISABELLA: Nothing can save her from the grief. She cannot escape it. She must suffer. And beyond the grief lies madness, the wide open ocean of despair.

(She throws herself at Guilio/Pantalone.)

ISABELLA: Have you seen my husband, signore? The one that I married I mean? I swear he was here, I saw him just here, but no, it was all a dream. *(To Arlecchino/ Simone.)* He told me he loved me back then, he gave me his heart with pride; but then he withdrew, and I never knew, he no longer stood by my side. *(To Leandro/*

Orazio.) For some of us love is a wish, for some it's a sport of youth; but some of us feel that love should be real, not fiction at all, but truth.

VITTORIA: *'For marriage is wonderful-'*

ISABELLA: The ocean is deep; down, down, down sinks the madwoman, singing all the way. *(She sings.)* She floats among memories, among visions, among voices. *(She quotes lines from the other characters, from throughout their lives together, impersonating them perfectly.)* And then one day, quite lost to the world, she arrives at the bottom of the ocean, the end of the world. She can go no deeper. She can rest.

(Isabella collapses. Huge applause. She is helped away. Backstage. Guilio and a furious Vittoria.)

VITTORIA: That was not my play. That was not my play. How dare she?

GUILIO: Calm down. Your play was a success.

(He is holding a bag of money.)

VITTORIA: I'm going to tear her hair from her sockets, where is she?

GUILIO: She's half out of her mind, thanks to you.

VITTORIA: Oh she knows exactly what she did. She's a player. She knows how to steal a scene. She knows how to steal a whole play.

GUILIO: You're paranoid.

VITTORIA: You're not a woman, you have no idea what we're capable of.

GUILIO: In your case, that's true.

VITTORIA: Excuse me. I made up a play, no more, no less.

GUILIO: A play in which a man cheats on his wife with a maid.

VITTORIA: A perfectly normal subject for a play.

GUILIO: How long have you known?

VITTORIA: I'm sure I have no idea what you're talking about.

GUILIO: Vittoria.

VITTORIA: Oh for God's sake. Everyone in this company is so idiotically blind. Ever since her stupid little speech about sentiment – don't you ever put two and two together? You're the company treasurer.

(Enter Francesco, Simone, Orazio, supporting Isabella. Sylvia leads them on.)

SYLVIA: Sit her down over here.

FRANCESCO: Get her some water, will you?

ORAZIO: It was magnificent. Magnificent. I was moved to tears.

FRANCESCO: Don't crowd her.

VITTORIA: Signora. I have never had the misfortune to play opposite a woman so conceited, so ignorant, and so selfish that she would hijack the course of a play for her own ends. There is such a thing as honor on the stage. The Duke was watching. You won't get away with this.

GUILIO: Can somebody calm her down?

ORAZIO: Vittoria, please.

VITTORIA: That was my play, mine, mine, MINE...

(The Duke of Mantua enters.)

VITTORIA: Oh Vincenzo... these nasty, nasty players – they have broken my heart into a hundred pieces...

DUKE: There there, peachblossom. The Grand Duke thought it was marvelous, especially the end.

VITTORIA: No! That wasn't my play. That was her making things up, the scene-stealing little bitch, the clap-hungry rat-faced narcissist –

DUKE: Is this true?

VITTORIA: I demand that you strike her name from the contract immediately. I demand it. Isabella Andreini will play no more for the Gelosi. Vincenzo. Vincenzo!

DUKE: *(producing contract)* Gelosi. Once again I must express my serious disappointment with your actions.

VITTORIA: A promising career cut short by an act of flagrant disrespect. Strike her name. Strike her name.

(Francesco grabs and tears up the contract.)

VITTORIA: What are you doing?

FRANCESCO: I'm tearing up this contract.

ORAZIO: Oh dear.

VITTORIA: That is our contract with Vincenzo.

FRANCESCO: It was.

VITTORIA: Do you see what he did? All of you? He just threw away our lives. For the second time. This philandering moron just threw away our lives. Are you going to stand for it? Orazio, do something. Do something you pusillanimous little twit. Guilio. Guilio, you sycophant, you mediocre penny-pinching moralist, do something. That's it. I am done with the Gelosi. I'm done. There are other companies. There are companies who would kill for a leading lady like me.

DUKE: Come, peachblossom. Come away.

VITTORIA: This company does not deserve me. You could have had me, you fools, instead of her, you could have had me. I would have led you to every Court in Europe. I would have been your first real first lady. The Gelosi, starring Vittoria Piissimi – the greatest – the best – the most celebrated – I want to be celebrated... Please...

(The Duke has pulled her off.)

GUILIO: *(of contract)* That was our life.

FRANCESCO: Guilio. I am sorry.

ORAZIO: Gelosi. You have all been good to me. Signora Andreini, I will think of you always with the deepest respect. But I cannot help it. I must live in hope, or I do not wish to live at all.

GUILIO: You're not going after that woman? She's a monster. You said it yourself.

ORAZIO: For some of us, signora, it is better to be devoured. I follow.

(He exits after Vittoria.)

SIMONE: He's out of his mind.

SYLVIA: *(to Isabella)* Signora. I don't expect you to forgive me; but I hope that an apology will make a difference.

ISABELLA: I won't forgive you, you're right. As for apologies; they so rarely live up to the mistakes that induce them. What you do means more to me than what you say.

SYLVIA: I understand, signora.

(Sylvia starts to collect her things. Guilio is counting money.)

FRANCESCO: How much?

GUILIO: Looks like around 400.

FRANCESCO: That will last us a few months.

GUILIO: If we're careful.

FRANCESCO: Plus money in the hat.

SIMONE: Sylvia, want to come and look around Florence?

SYLVIA: All right.

SIMONE: You don't need your bags.

SYLVIA: I do.

(She has all her things.)

SIMONE: Back soon.

SYLVIA: Goodbye signora, signori.

FRANCESCO: Goodbye.

(Sylvia and Simone, whistling, exit. Guilio counts money.)

FRANCESCO: Isabella. What can I do?

ISABELLA: Fetch me my parchment and quill.

FRANCESCO: Isabella - I will never leave your side.

GUILIO: Fifty one, fifty two, fifty three...

4. POVERTY

(Many months later. It is snowing. Francesco, Guilio, Simone in skirt are rehearsing.)

PANTALONE (GUILIO): *'Flaminia? Won't you stand a little closer, my precious Flaminia?'*

FLAMINIA (SIMONE): *'Oh Pantalone. I don't know if I should...'*

PANTALONE (GUILIO): *'Give me a kiss, my sweet little Flaminia.'*

FRANCESCO: *(interrupting)* Just a moment. Simone, what's the matter?

SIMONE: It's too cold to rehearse.

FRANCESCO: We have to rehearse. We have a performance this afternoon.

SIMONE: All right, all right.

(They are about to begin.)

SIMONE: I feel ridiculous in this skirt.

FRANCESCO: I remember.

SIMONE: Perhaps the signora feels better by now.

FRANCESCO: She needs to rest.

SIMONE: She's always resting. She's been resting for months. Some playing would do her good.

FRANCESCO: She won't do it.

SIMONE: She was better than the rest of us put together.

GUILIO: He may be right.

FRANCESCO: I know.

SIMONE: Come a bit closer. Warm me up. I can't rehearse till I'm warm.

(They huddle together.)

FRANCESCO: I miss prison.

GUILIO: What?

FRANCESCO: I miss it. We knew where we were.

SIMONE: I know what you mean.

GUILIO: You're both mad.

FRANCESCO: Come on. Admit it, you miss it too.

GUILIO: We were tortured! All right, maybe a little bit.

FRANCESCO: Told you.

(Pause.)

SIMONE: We were the Gelosi. Remember?

(Pause.)

FRANCESCO: How many coins do we have left?

GUILIO: Twelve.

FRANCESCO: Can't even afford a doctor.

GUILIO: We'll earn a few more this afternoon.

SIMONE: I don't have to have any dinner.

FRANCESCO: It's all right, Simone. Thank you.

(Pause.)

SIMONE: *(to Francesco)* You should never have married her. You didn't love her.

FRANCESCO: Of course I loved her.

SIMONE: You stood there and told me you didn't love her. You told me.

FRANCESCO: I didn't know that I loved her. But I loved her.

SIMONE: Well I hope she knows it now.

FRANCESCO: I don't know what she knows. I try. In the middle of the night – I wake up, she's muttering to herself, writing things down. I whisper to her. I touch her neck...

GUILIO: *(cackling)* You never had much skill with women.

FRANCESCO: Hey.

GUILIO: You didn't. You had luck, but you never had any skill. Very different things.

SIMONE: I asked Sylvia to kiss me once. We were walking in Florence. We walked all day. By the time we got as far as the church of Santa Felicita, the moon had come out. Look, Sylvia. The moon is made of cheese. One day we will walk on it, you and I. Can I sing you a song? And then I asked her to kiss me.

FRANCESCO: What did she do?

SIMONE: She told me to close my eyes. Like this.

FRANCESCO: And?

SIMONE: I waited. The happiest few moments of my life. When I opened my eyes, she was gone. I never saw her again.

(Pause.)

SIMONE: *(to Francesco)* If you had to do it all again, would you do it all the same?

FRANCESCO: No.

SIMONE: Maybe that's what she needs to know.

(Isabella enters, with a stack of papers.)

ISABELLA: Francesco.

FRANCESCO: Yes, my darling.

ISABELLA: Help me put these in order, will you? I keep dropping the papers - and I can't read my own writing...

FRANCESCO: Of course, my darling.

(She collapses. The papers spill everywhere.)

FRANCESCO: Isabella!

(They all go to her.)

FRANCESCO: I think you should go back in the wagon and lie down.

ISABELLA: I'm all right. I just need to walk for a moment.

(She recovers. Guilio and Simone withdraw.)

FRANCESCO: Isabella. You remember you asked me once, what was it for. The stage, I mean. And I didn't tell you what I really thought.

ISABELLA: Yes, Francesco, I remember.

FRANCESCO: But now I am telling you the truth. I've changed my mind. You were right. Nothing I did was anything more than a stick thrown at a tree, it made no difference. The world is the same. I wish I had listened to you, Isabella. I wish I had stuck to beauty and truth; I wish I had followed you.

ISABELLA: I've changed my mind too, Francesco.

FRANCESCO: What do you mean?

ISABELLA: She was right. When she said it was all a lie. She was right; every word I ever wrote was a lie. Read my plays – read my poems - you can't deny it. Fabrications. And the other one was right, too, when she called it all sentiment. Women really are far more intelligent than men. Yes. I have poured out my heart in sentiment and lies. I am no different from any other player that will ever walk the stage.

FRANCESCO: Isabella...

ISABELLA: 'If ever there is anyone who reads / These my neglected poems, don't believe / In their feigned ardors... The Muses inspiration I have / Set forth with lies.' I think I will lie down now, Francesco.

(She lies in his arms.)

FRANCESCO: Isabella, I love you. I love you.

ISABELLA: Let the snow be my blanket, my darling. Let the snow be my blanket for now.

(Isabella is dying.)

FRANCESCO: *(remembering Isabella's lines)*
'You cannot capture our hearts
Unless you, too, leave the earth behind,
As if in a dream, a slow dream; it is the one
Condition of love.'

EPILOGUE

FRANCESCO: Signori, here our story ends. The Gelosi died along with my wife. Simone returned to Bologna, where he lived with his mother and became a cheesemonger. Guilio joined another company, and made a good living. I devoted myself to the publication of Isabella's writing, and I managed it; she was declared a member of the Academy of Letters in 1601. If you go to an old library in Italy, you might still find her plays. That's it. We have no more to tell you. We're all dead now. Long dead.

(The company are gathered at the front of the stage.)

FRANCESCO: You have witnessed it all. Most of it is just how it happened, and as for the rest – you'll never know any better. We've done our best. Thanks for your patience. You can go home now. But we hope, above all else, that as you go about your business, you remember the Gelosi. What do we believe in, after all? Why do we come here?

GUILIO: Profit.

VITTORIA: Fame.

ORAZIO: Love.

SIMONE: Food.

SYLVIA: Rebellion.

ISABELLA: Poetry.

FRANCESCO: Revenge. We come for revenge.

(Muted disagreement. The company Gelosi drift off to their places in the shadows. They will be back again tomorrow night.)

THE END

NOTES

NOTES

NOTES

Made in the USA
Middletown, DE
24 July 2024